I0759774

BRIGID EHRMANTRAUT is an expert in Celtic languages and literature, and is Associate Lecturer in Latin and in the History of the British Isles at the University of St Andrews. She studied Classics at Princeton University and received her PhD in Anglo-Saxon, Norse and Celtic from the University of Cambridge. Prior to joining the School of History at St Andrews, she held a Research Fellowship at St John's College, Cambridge. She is also the author of *Classical Myth in Medieval Ireland* (Boydell and Brewer, 2025).

BRIGID EHRMANTRAUT

CELTIC MAGIC

A PRACTITIONER'S GUIDE

With 106 illustrations

To my grandparents.

FRONTISPIECE: Head from the temple pediment of Sulis Minerva at Bath. It has been identified variously as a gorgon, a local water god and Oceanus.

First published in the United Kingdom in 2026 by
Thames & Hudson Ltd, 6–24 Britannia Street, London WC1X 9JD

First published in the United States of America in 2026 by
Thames & Hudson Inc., 500 Fifth Avenue, New York, New York 10110

Cover illustrations by Petra Börner

EU Authorized Representative: Interart S.A.R.L.
19 rue Charles Auray, 93500 Pantin, Paris, France
productsafety@thameshudson.co.uk
interart.fr

A CIP catalogue record for this book is available from the British Library

Library of Congress Control Number 2025938786

ISBN 978-0-500-02973-2

01

Printed and bound in China by Shanghai Offset Printing Products Limited

CONTENTS

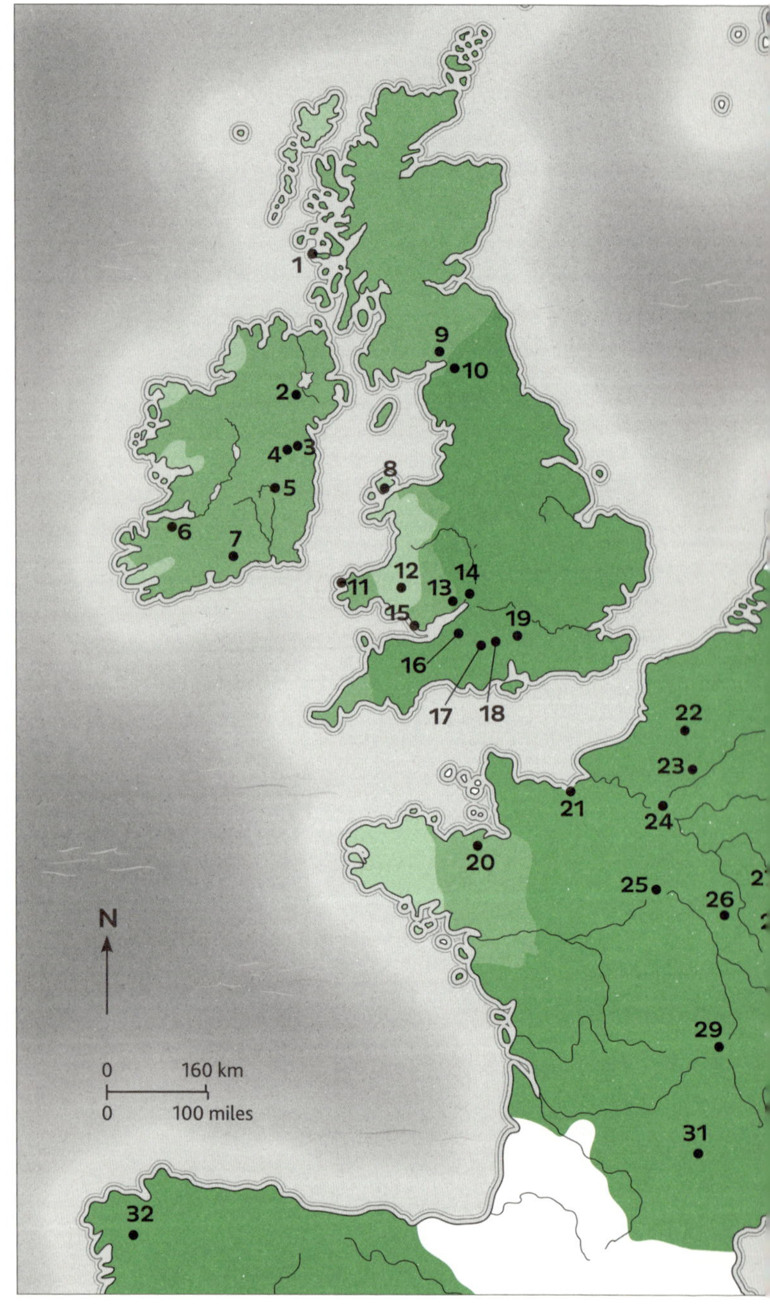

1
2
3
4
5
6
7
8
9
10
11
12
13
14
15
16
17
18
19
20
21
22
23
24
25
26
29
31
32
N
0
160 km
0
100 miles

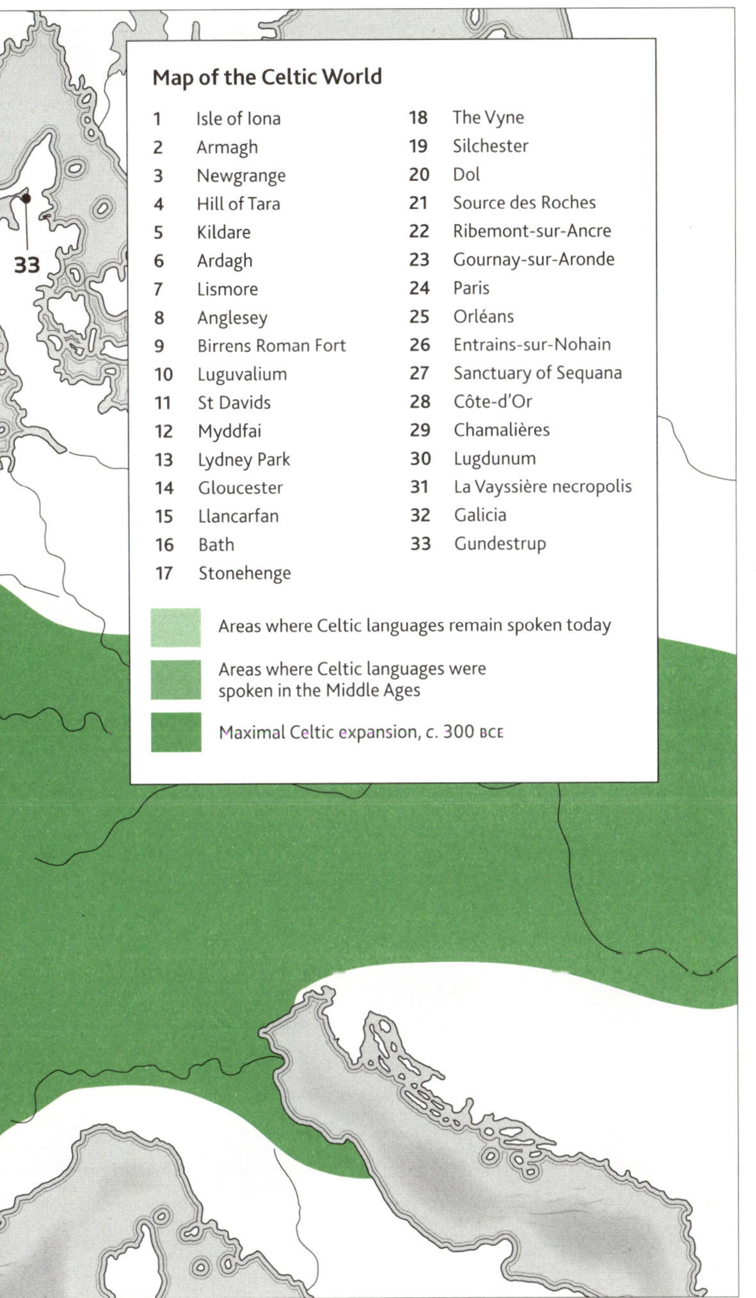
33
Map of the Celtic World
1 Isle of Iona
2 Armagh
3 Newgrange
4 Hill of Tara
5 Kildare
6 Ardagh
7 Lismore
8 Anglesey
9 Birrens Roman Fort
10 Luguvalium
11 St Davids
12 Myddfai
13 Lydney Park
14 Gloucester
15 Llancarfan
16 Bath
17 Stonehenge
18 The Vyne
19 Silchester
20 Dol
21 Source des Roches
22 Ribemont-sur-Ancre
23 Gournay-sur-Aronde
24 Paris
25 Orléans
26 Entrains-sur-Nohain
27 Sanctuary of Sequana
28 Côte-d'Or
29 Chamalières
30 Lugdunum
31 La Vayssière necropolis
32 Galicia
33 Gundestrup
Areas where Celtic languages remain spoken today
Areas where Celtic languages were spoken in the Middle Ages
Maximal Celtic expansion, c. 300 BCE

INTRODUCTION

Britain, an imaginary 5th century CE.

A great battle has been fought and the dead are too many to count. The king of Britain, Aurelius, wonders what is to be done with them. He turns to Merlin, who advises the king that if he wishes to build a memorial that will last forever then he must go to Ireland and fetch the Giants' Ring, a circle of huge stones. Merlin recounts that the stones were originally brought from Africa to Ireland by ancient giants who used them to build a miraculous healing bath. Now they cannot be moved by anyone, except through genius or art. Aurelius laughs, but Merlin assures him it can be done.

In Ireland, Aurelius's brother Uther Pendragon and his men try to move the stones. But they cannot so much as budge them. Pulleys, ropes and ladders – the men's instruments fail them. Now it is Merlin's turn to laugh. He uses his own devices and the stones come down easily and are loaded onto ships bound for Britain.

We all know the magician Merlin. Advisor to King Arthur. Enchanter extraordinaire. Prophet. Seer. Sorcerer. Or at least we think we do. The story of how Merlin moved the stones from Ireland to their current home at Stonehenge in southern Britain is a classic example of Celtic magic. But upon closer inspection, is it really magic? Or even Celtic?

The story is based on Geoffrey of Monmouth's *History of the Kings of Britain*, written in the 12th century CE. Geoffrey was writing in Latin and, while he claimed to make use of an ancient book 'in the British tongue', this supposed source has yet to be identified (if it ever existed). Geoffrey is associated with Monmouth on the border between Wales and England but there is no evidence one way or another that he himself was Welsh or spoke Welsh (or, indeed, any other Celtic languages). His Merlin is a composite of several characters who already existed in literature, including a Welsh poet and wildman named Myrddin, a fictionalized Roman commander and a boy who was said to have supernatural powers. Despite early modern theories about Celtic druids and Stonehenge, we know today that Stonehenge is a Neolithic monument that was built around 2500 BCE, long before any speakers of a Celtic language lived in Britain.

Stonehenge has meant many things to many people over time, including William Blake, who interprets it here as a druidic temple, 1834–1921.

Nevertheless, Geoffrey's account proved very popular, and for centuries his versions of Merlin and Arthur have influenced nearly all subsequent appearances of these characters in stories appearing in both Latin and the vernacular (the commonly spoken languages of everyday people; in this case not Latin, which was usually the preserve of religious and social elites during the Middle Ages). Can we say that this muddle of sources, languages and characters is Celtic?

How about magic? Merlin is best known today as a great magician but does he actually use magic to move the stones of Stonehenge to Britain? Geoffrey never tells us if Merlin's 'devices' are magic as such or merely innate skill and clever use of technology. All he reports is that Merlin gets the men to move the stones to the harbour while normal ships transport the cargo back to Britain. We are left wondering whether our classic tale of a Celtic enchanter magically moving ancient stones is really Celtic or magical at all...

Clearly something needs to be said about what we mean by the terms 'Celtic' and 'magic' before we go any further. In this book, 'Celtic' refers primarily to the language family, which includes Gaulish, Celtiberian, Welsh, Breton, Cornish, Irish, Scottish Gaelic and Manx, among others, and to texts produced in these languages or in multilingual environments in which these languages were used. We are not necessarily using it to mean the diverse range of material culture, political organization and self-identification of Celtic language speakers, ancient or modern. Indeed, most medieval Irish speakers would not have known that their language was closely related to Welsh, much less to the languages spoken by the people that Julius Caesar was fighting in Gaul (roughly, modern-day France) in the 1st century BCE. The definition of Celtic here is limited and linguistic, and because the survival rate of evidence from the ancient and medieval periods is poor, this book will deal primarily with written texts, be they brief curse inscriptions carved onto lead tablets, charms written in the margins of later manuscripts, or longer works of medieval literature.

'Magic' is also tricky to define. For most ancient and medieval people, both Celtic speakers and non-Celtic speakers, magic was not significantly different from religion, nature or simply how they saw the world around them. Even for many people today, magic is a somewhat slippery concept. Do you practise magic when you avoid stepping on cracks in the pavement to avoid misfortune or knock on wood to ensure good luck? Because magic is so difficult to define and because it means different things to different people (and probably always has), this book does not attempt to offer a firm definition. The Oxford English Dictionary defines magic as: 'The use of ritual activities or observances which are intended to influence the course of events or to manipulate the natural world, usually involving the use of an occult or secret body of knowledge'. This book will work loosely with this definition with a focus on the activities that regular people might have practised on a daily basis. It is, of course, difficult to tell how much occult or secret knowledge premodern magic involved since, by definition, such knowledge was secret!

This is a book in two halves: the first part deals with magic in the ancient Celtic-speaking world, while the second looks at magic from the medieval period in areas where Celtic languages were spoken. Our ancient evidence comes from epigraphy (inscriptions on a hard, durable material such as stone or metal) and from classical Greek and Roman written accounts about their Celtic-speaking neighbours (not all of which are trustworthy). For the Middle Ages, we have longer narratives and historical texts involving magic that survive in manuscripts written in Irish, Welsh and Latin, as well as prayers, charms and medical recipes. The two halves of this book represent both a chronological and a geographic divide. While the earlier material comes from continental Europe (especially Gaul) and from Britain during the Roman period, our medieval Celtic language sources are largely from Wales and Ireland from about the 7th to 14th centuries CE.

A curse tablet made in southern France in the 1st century CE and a medical ritual written down in Wales in the 13th century may share a common language family (in the same way that the English, German and Norwegian languages do) and they both might invoke magical powers in loosely similar ways, but very little beyond that directly connects them.

Magical texts and objects from Gaul and Roman Britain rarely come with instructions. Archaeologists have found dedications to Celtic gods from throughout the ancient world and have excavated curse inscriptions that were cast into water or placed in tombs. But, as we will see in the first part of this book, the challenge is working out how someone was supposed to pray to one of these gods or which magic words or ritual gestures accompanied a curse. Ancient Celtic languages like Gaulish are difficult to read, even for experts, and not enough of these languages survive for us to be able to translate surviving ancient Celtic inscriptions in the same way we can with Greek and Latin, although we can make educated guesses. Sometimes it is unclear whether a curse is directed against thieves, legal opponents or romantic rivals.... We can find out more information about the religions and magic of ancient Celtic speakers (including lurid depictions of bloody human sacrifice) from classical authors who wrote about them in Greek and Latin – but most of the time we have only their word to go on.

The medieval material in Part II is from Celtic-speaking areas, including Wales and Ireland, which were thoroughly Christian by this period. It is thus important to realize that, for the most part, medieval magic was not incompatible with Christianity: it was simply another form of Christian devotion. We often cannot be sure whether medieval magical charms had some pre-Christian precedent because we lack early written sources that demonstrate clear continuity. The second part of the book will therefore consider medieval material in its Christian context and what it can tell us

Merlin (left) and King Arthur (centre) have a debate in this illustration from a 14th-century French manuscript.

about real medieval people and their daily lives, rather than about some hypothetical pagan past.

At the same time, medieval Irish and Welsh literature abounds with narratives set in the pre-Christian past featuring magical people, places and things. From the Otherworldly *síd* mounds that feature prominently in medieval Irish tales to magicians in medieval Welsh literature who can transform people into animals and create life out of flowers, magic suffuses stories and landscapes. Slighted poets utter incantations and bloodthirsty beings ride the winds at night and feast on the blood of dead warriors. This literary vision of the past is the product of creative medieval authors and must be clearly distinguished from the much more poorly attested historical realities of pre-Christian religions and magical practices in Celtic-speaking areas.

This, then, is a book that is as much about what we *don't know* about magic in the Celtic past as about what we *do know* about it. How ancient Celtic speakers in Gaul and Britain thought magic worked, what most magic rituals involved, and to what degree magical practices might have differed from place to place or time to time remain something of a mystery. However, we do have a few glimpses of the steps that specific ancient Celtic speakers took to practise magic and we have examples of the magical texts they produced. Although very little is currently known about the religions of pre-Christian Ireland or how many (if any) pagan beliefs survived into the later Christian period, we have evidence that medieval Irish and Welsh Christians wrote everyday prayers and healing charms and included magic in literary works. These were real people and the magic they performed and wrote about was important to them and helped them understand and control their constantly changing world.

This book is intended to be a practical guide to the types of magic practised by Celtic speakers from antiquity through the Middle Ages (to the extent that this is possible to know). It will focus on real-world people and real-world magic. Readers can even try some of these magical spells and rituals at home. Discover how to curse your enemies, recite a charm to keep demonic powers at bay, learn a spell to open all the barrels of ale in a hall and, if you overindulge in the results, try a medieval hangover cure! But please perform your magic responsibly. We cannot be held liable for the results.

PART I

ANCIENT MAGIC

1

DEITIES AND DEDICATIONS

Paris, 6 March 1711.

The cathedral of Notre-Dame de Paris reaches to the skies. But underground, its crypts are also reaching deeper and deeper. In 1711, the choir is being redesigned and a crypt excavated beneath for the burials of former archbishops. The space is small and the air is thick with dust. One of the workmen lifting up floor tiles and old stones sneezes. The work is hard and he blinks sweat out of his eyes. An old wall runs beneath the cathedral and the excavation is heavy going. The mortar is difficult to demolish, even with the assistance of iron wedges and large mallets. The workman and his companions get barely half a metre in before finding another wall nearly a metre thick. This wall is older and the rubble is easier to remove. Eagerly, the man pulls away a row of rubble. Then another.

He is greeted by a pair of ancient eyes.

They have not seen the light of day in one-and-a-half thousand years.

THE PILLAR OF THE BOATMEN

When you think of the cathedral of Notre-Dame in Paris in all its Gothic glory, ancient Gaulish gods are probably not the first thing that comes to mind. However, when a new crypt was built under the cathedral in 1711 excavators found blocks from a 1st-century CE pillar dedicated to a group of Gaulish and Roman deities. The pillar

The Roman god Jove (Jupiter) looks on from the Pillar of the Boatmen.

was set up by a guild of local boatmen and was probably originally located along the River Seine near docks used for trading. The monument's blocks were subsequently reused in the 3rd or 4th century CE to shore up the walls around the Île de la Cité, protecting the island from attack. The banks of the Seine have moved over the intervening years, however, so what was once the edge of the docks and later the location of the defensive walls is now located underneath Notre-Dame.

The monument is known as the Pillar of the Boatmen after its sailor patrons and is now located in the Musée de Cluny in Paris.

An inscription on one of the blocks declares that it was 'Set up in public by the sailors of Paris' and dedicated 'to Tiberius Caesar Augustus [and] Jove the Best and Greatest'. This is very helpful because it tells us who commissioned it and that it was made during the reign of the Roman emperor Tiberius who ruled 14–37 CE. Having such a firm date is unusual, compared to the other inscriptions and texts discussed in this book – many of our textual sources for ancient and medieval Celtic material do not give us the names of the people who produced them, let alone the dates at which they were written.

The Pillar of the Boatmen consists of four rectangular blocks. Each face of each block depicts a god or group of gods to whom the pillar is also dedicated, for a total of sixteen scenes (although the lower sections of each block are now fragmentary). About two-thirds of these images are accompanied by inscriptions that identify the god(s) in question by name. It is reasonably common to find images of Greco-Roman deities accompanied by their names, but the Pillar of the Boatmen is one of only a few surviving monuments that both name and depict Celtic gods. Most of the ancient evidence for Celtic deities is either visual or epigraphic, so it is often difficult to match up images of gods with their names and attributes.

One of the most interesting things about the Pillar of the Boatmen is that it includes both Roman and Gaulish deities. Clearly these gods were being worshipped together by the same group of people. We might imagine that some members of the boatmen's guild had their own favourite gods, possibly based on their own family history or cultural identity but, of course, this did not mean they did not also worship the other gods. Indeed, the people who made and paid for the pillar probably didn't think of these gods as belonging to different religions or being fundamentally different in character. For the polytheistic boatmen living and working in Paris in the 1st century CE, all of these divine beings were powerful and could be invoked when needed.

Who are the deities depicted on the Pillar of the Boatmen?

Roman gods include:

- Jove: Roman father of the gods, associated with thunder and the heavens, and the main dedicatee of the pillar
- Vulcan: the Roman god of fire and metalworking (smiths), often compared to the Greek Hephaestus
- Fortuna: Roman goddess of fortune
- Castor and Pollux: a pair of mythical heroic twins sometimes associated with battles or oath swearing in Rome (a very similar-looking but fragmentary figure on another side of the pillar may be Castor's brother Pollux).

While Gaulish deities listed are:

- Cernunnos
- Smertrios
- Esus
- Taruos Trigaranus
- Eurises
- Senan[...].

Other sections of the pillar are now damaged and missing any text they may have once had, so it is possible that other Roman gods including Juno, Mars, Venus, Mercury and the Celtic goddess Rosmerta (a goddess of abundance often associated with Mercury) were originally depicted on these now-fragmentary sides as well, but it is hard to tell today.

Cernunnos on the Pillar of the Boatmen, complete with horns, torcs and an air of mystery.

Cernunnos appears as a man with a pair of antlers (perhaps unsurprisingly since his name is related to the Gaulish word for 'horn'). A ring or torc (a type of neck or arm-ring known from Iron Age Europe) hangs from each antler. The figure is probably seated as there is not enough space on the lower section of the block for his legs (if they were originally as long as those of the figures on other sides of the block), but the block is worn away here. Human figures with antlers (sometimes in seated positions) appear in art and epigraphy across northwestern Europe and these are often assumed to represent the same deity. However, the Pillar of the Boatmen is the only known place where the name Cernunnos is found with an accompanying image, so we simply do not know whether any of the other horned figures represent the same god or not, or if they were just worshipped in a similar way. One particularly famous horned figure, also depicted in a seated position and carrying a torc, appears

A figure with antlers appears on the interior of the Gundestrup Cauldron. This figure's connection to Cernunnos remains unknown.

on the Gundestrup Cauldron, which was found in 1891 in a bog in Denmark. Scholarly opinions have varied greatly about the date and origin of the cauldron, although current scholarship suggests that it was made sometime in the 1st century BCE in Thrace, near the Black Sea. The Gundestrup Cauldron is a beautiful and evocative artefact and it is no wonder that people have tried to connect it with mythological traditions across Iron Age Europe. However, in the absence of other more conclusive textual or archaeological evidence it is not a particularly helpful source for us in understanding the religions of the boatmen of 1st-century CE Paris.

Smertrios is depicted on the pillar as a bearded man facing a snake while holding a club (or at least a stick-like object, the end of which is now damaged). His name is familiar because it appears elsewhere in ancient Gaul and Germany, sometimes in conjunction with the Roman god of war Mars as 'Mars Smertrios'. This phenomenon by which a deity from one culture was expressed as a manifestation of another deity from a different culture is called 'syncretism'. The name Mars Smertrios, which appears in dedications from Möhn and Liesenich in modern-day southwestern Germany, thus represents syncretism between the Roman god Mars and the Celtic god Smertrios. Syncretism usually happens when the deities in question are similar in some respect, so we may conjecture that Celtic Smertrios and Roman Mars shared some martial associations or were especially popular among soldiers. Such examples of Gallo-Roman and Romano-British syncretism are common. Smertrios's club and the snake he faces also recall another Greek and Roman figure: Hercules. Hercules was very popular throughout the ancient Mediterranean world and so it is possible that the Paris boatmen also saw their god as a Celtic parallel to the Greco-Roman mythological hero.

Esus appears on one face of the pillar holding a blade in the act of cutting down a tree. Among the Gaulish gods on the monument Esus is surprisingly well-attested elsewhere: his name also appears on a statue from Trier in modern-day Germany, as a component of several Gaulish personal names, and in the classical Latin poet Lucan's epic poem *Pharsalia*. Lucan implies that human victims were sacrificed to Esus but, as we shall explore in greater depth, classical authors were not necessarily reliable sources for Gaulish religion. Even if there is some truth behind Lucan's account, it almost certainly does not reflect the worship of Esus in Romanized 1st-century Gaul when the Pillar of the Boatmen was made.

Taruos Trigaranus (literally Gaulish for 'Three Crane Bull') is perhaps the most mysterious figure named on the pillar. As the name suggests, this side of the pillar does indeed portray a bull and three cranes. Two cranes stand on the bull's back and one on its head. A tree (like the one Esus is felling) appears in the background. Any mythic narrative to which the name Taruos Trigaranus or the image

Taruos Trigaranus ('Three Crane Bull') on the Pillar of the Boatmen.

on the pillar may allude is now lost, however, and we have only this enigmatic picture to puzzle over.

Other named groups appear about whom we know even less: three armed men with beards are labelled the Eurises on one side, while three even more poorly preserved figures wearing robes on another side are called the Senan[...] (the rest is fragmentary and the transcription is disputed). These may be gods or local people, perhaps even some of the boatmen who dedicated the monument.

But does the pillar count as a type of magic? Most people in the ancient world would not have drawn a clear distinction between 'magic' and 'religion'. Unlike some of the curse tablets that we will encounter, the inscriptions on the Pillar of the Boatmen do not ask the gods for any particular favours. That said, it's probably a safe assumption that the boatmen's guild wanted to thank their gods and expected some kind of divine goodwill in return for paying for the pillar. In this regard the boatmen's choice to erect the monument conforms to our very broad definition of magic as ritual behaviour intended to 'influence the course of events or to manipulate the natural world'. Further rituals might have accompanied the process of setting up the pillar – it has been suggested that instead of forming one tall column, the blocks were supposed to be arranged into two lower altars upon which offerings could be made. In addition, the pillar was a civic monument that not only demonstrated the piety of the boatmen's guild, but also served as a testament to their wealth and ability to commission fine stonework on a large scale. The pillar might have been erected on the location of a cult site or temple, in which case, like the much later medieval cathedral of Notre-Dame, it would have glorified the object(s) of worship while showing off the wealth and skill of the builders. It also marked the location of the boatmen's wharfs and showed off their importance to passersby. In this respect, we could think of the pillar as a piece of public art or even as some form of publicity for the boatmen themselves.

GODS AND GODDESSES

One of the surprising things about the Pillar of the Boatmen is that it does not depict any of the better-known Celtic gods. Beyond Gaul, a number of Celtic deities turn up repeatedly, indicating that their worship was widespread among Celtic speakers. In some cases, the Romanized versions of such cults proved popular throughout the Roman world. The names of deities such as the god Lugus and the goddess Brigantia appear in inscriptions and placenames from Spain to Britain to Switzerland. Cities throughout the Roman Empire were named after Lugus, including Lyon in modern-day France (which was Latinized as *Lugdunum* and originally meant 'the fort of Lugus' in Gaulish) and Carlisle in northwestern England (originally Romano-British *Luguvalium*, meaning '[city] of the strength of Lugus'). However, we know little about Lugus himself. One inscription from Galicia, Spain tells us that he was worshipped by shoemakers, but this doesn't really tell us anything more than knowing that the gods on the Pillar of the Boatmen were worshipped by sailors. Scholars often compare Lugus to the Roman gods Mercury and Apollo and identify statues of youthful male deities from Celtic-speaking areas as Lugus, Mercury or Apollo. Based on the images alone without accompanying text, however, it can be tricky to tell which god(s) we're actually dealing with.

Often our best evidence for how Celtic gods were worshipped and what people believed about them comes from syncretism with Greco-Roman deities. For instance, in inscriptions from Roman Britain, Brigantia is syncretized with Roman goddesses associated with battle and military success, like Minerva and Victoria, and she is sometimes paired with the Roman god Jupiter. An image of Brigantia from a Roman fort in Birrens in Dumfriesshire, Scotland depicts the goddess with the iconography of Minerva, including her helmet, spear and aegis featuring the head of a Gorgon. Evidence like this from Roman military forts in Britain is not surprising since soldiers tended to worship martial

The goddess Brigantia is shown with Minerva's spear and helmet in a statue found at Birrens, 120–180 CE.

deities, whether local, Roman or a syncretized combination of the two. The Celtic-speaking Brigantes people who lived in the region were especially fond of their patron goddess (from whom they derived their name) but worship of Brigantia was not limited to the locals. Soldiers from other parts of the empire stationed at the fort likely recognized her kinship to Minerva, their goddess of war, strategy and engineering.

The sculpture of Brigantia at Birrens bears an inscription declaring that 'Amandus, the engineer, fulfilled the order by command'. Amandus was an engineer in the Roman army who set up the sculpture at the direction of a *collegium* (or guild) of other worshippers, seeking to win favour with the goddess for his compatriots and himself. Like the sailors' guild in Paris who were responsible for the Pillar of the Boatmen, worshippers believed that the acts of paying for and creating the statue would bring them divine rewards. They might have left offerings to the goddess at this sculpture or at a nearby altar. The image of Brigantia at Birrens was found alongside a dedication to the Roman emperor and Mercury in a stone building slightly west of the main Roman fort. This location may have been more accessible to both local and military worshippers than a shrine in the fort itself would have been, or alternatively, perhaps the land here was just available.

Similar examples of syncretism can be found in the worship of the Gaulish god Belenus, who we didn't meet under Notre-Dame but who pops up in an inscription from Burgundy as 'Apollo Belenus'. Local worshippers clearly thought that Belenus shared important features with the Greco-Roman Apollo, in this case probably associations with medicine and healing. The goddess Sirona also appears alongside Apollo in inscriptions found along the Danube River and she probably had a healing cult as well. Sirona's iconography often includes snakes and eggs, much like the Greco-Roman goddess of health Hygieia. The snakes and eggs may have been borrowed wholesale from Hygieia's cult or they may have already been associated with Sirona to some degree. Either way, it is clear that the communities who worshipped Sirona were multicultural and had plenty of exposure to deities from Greece and Rome. In an inscription from Switzerland, the Gaulish deity Sucellus is amalgamated with the Roman god Silvanus, who was associated with forests, as well as with fields and property boundaries. The goddess Rosmerta frequently appears alongside the Roman god Mercury or with iconography associated with him. Rosmerta, who is often depicted holding a cornucopia or *patera* (a shallow dish), has been linked to abundance and fertility. The Syrian satirist Lucian (writing in Greek in the 2nd century CE) claimed that the Gaulish deity Ogmios was another version of Hercules. In Lucian's account, Ogmios appears with Hercules's lion skin and club. Unlike Hercules, however, he is described as a wizened old man who leads a group of captives by golden leashes that are attached to the ears of the captives and to the god's tongue. A Gaul in the story claims that the golden leashes are there because Ogmios is also the god of eloquence. Lucian was a satirist, so perhaps we ought

Minerva with her own spear, helmet and shield with Medusa motif, from a 17th-century engraving.

not to take his account literally, however... Ogmios also appears in two curse tablets from Raetia (modern Austria), but these do not mention Hercules.

All of this does not mean that Gaulish gods were always simply duplicates of Roman ones – in reality, correspondences between Gaulish and Greco-Roman deities were rarely ever one-to-one. It is just that most epigraphic information about Gaulish gods comes from Latin (or in some cases Greek) inscriptions, which were produced in multilingual communities by people familiar with Greco-Roman culture and religion. Additionally, syncretic thinking meant that similarities tended to be emphasized rather than differences. Plenty of Celtic deities turn up in inscriptions that do not mention Greco-Roman gods at all or turn up only as images without accompanying text, but in the absence of longer texts or Greco-Roman comparisons, it is much harder to say anything concrete about these examples.

Like Taruos Trigaranus on the Pillar of the Boatmen, these deities can only stare silently back at us out of the past.

A good example of a well-attested Gaulish goddess who is known primarily from Roman contexts is Epona. Her name is clearly Celtic and is related to a word meaning 'horse'. She is often found accompanied by horses in her iconography. Dedications to Epona and depictions of the goddess can be found from modern-day Portugal all the way to Romania – she was well-travelled because the Roman army adopted her as a favourite deity and troops took her with them across Europe. Her associations with horses apparently appealed to Roman cavalry soldiers of diverse ethnic and geographic origins, as is evident from an inscription to Epona from Germany dedicated by a Syrian soldier. It is unclear whether a Syrian stationed in Germany would have thought of Epona as a 'Gaulish' goddess any more than the boatmen who set up the pillar in Paris would have thought of Cernunnos and Vulcan as belonging to different cultures, peoples, languages or religions. Unlike some of the other Gaulish gods we have met, Epona rarely appears syncretized with Greco-Roman gods. Perhaps hers was a sphere of patronage that was not well represented among existing Greco-Roman deities. Eventually she became so thoroughly assimilated into Greco-Roman culture that she was no longer considered a foreign god in need of decoding with the help of a more familiar deity. The fact that Epona's worship was highly mobile thanks to the movements of the Roman legions across the empire probably helped her become a universal rather than local deity. As with the worship of Brigantia at Birrens, soldiers set up altars and sculptures of Epona in order to receive her favour in their military endeavours or thank her for help in the past. These dedications demonstrated their piety to the deity, to their fellow soldiers, and to others who might visit their monuments in the future. Soldiers and other people passing by such an altar later could have left their own offerings or said a quiet prayer. If you couldn't afford an altar, you could leave a small statue of the goddess in a sacred site or bring

Copper statue of Epona and two ponies from Romano-British Wiltshire.

it with you for luck on the road. Even without an expensive dedication or offering, you could keep the goddess close to you.

There is often a temptation to compare characters from medieval literature written in later Celtic languages such as Old Irish and Middle Welsh with these ancient Celtic gods about whom we often know very little. Scholars have observed that heroes, saints and supernatural figures in medieval Irish and Welsh literature bear names that are cognates (words that are descended from a common root word) with some of the names of deities worshipped in Gaul or Roman Britain. Some people have excitedly compared the dedication to Lugus by Galician shoemakers with a story from the medieval Welsh tale *Fourth Branch of the Mabinogi* in which the character Lleu works as a cobbler, and numerous proposals for a connection between the Romano-British goddess Brigantia and the Irish St Brigit have been proffered. This sort of identification is an uncertain and often fraught enterprise, however, because of the gulfs of time and space between

How to dedicate a temple to a Gaulish goddess and a Roman emperor

This formula is based on a Latin dedication to Epona and the emperor Augustus, found in Entrains-sur-Nohain, Nièvre, Bourgogne-Franche-Comté, France, dating to about the beginning of the 2nd century CE. The original donor was named Connonius son of Icotasgus, but you can substitute your own name and try it out yourself. (If you don't have the time or resources to build a full-sized temple, perhaps start with an altar or plaque.)

> *Sacred to Augustus and the goddess Epona, [your name here] gave a temple with all its decorations willingly from their own merit [i.e. at their own expense].*

the ancient, mostly continental evidence and the medieval literary narratives of Britain and Ireland. What might look like religious continuity between ancient gods and medieval sources could simply be the reappearances of relatively common names or motifs. Think, for instance, about how many people today are named Denise, Denis or Denny or a variation thereof. This does not mean they are all intentionally named after the ancient Greek god of wine, Dionysus, even though this is the origin of their names. Even if medieval literary characters do represent some continuation of the pre-Christian past, most medieval authors and audiences were probably not aware of this, so we cannot use their literary creations to reconstruct belief systems from a thousand or more years before. Brigit can only tell us about Brigit, not about Brigantia.

SEEKING CURES AT THE SOURCE OF THE SEINE

The inscriptions and dedications we have seen so far give us some idea about which divine beings Celtic speakers and their neighbours worshipped, but they do not necessarily tell us a lot about what kinds of things people wanted from their gods and goddesses or how they went about getting whatever it was they wanted. Seeking one source of information about what daily ritual activities entailed, we arrive at another source, that of the River Seine in Côte-d'Or, Bourgogne-Franche-Comté, in modern-day France (a good deal upstream from where the boatmen set up their Pillar in Paris). The Seine derives its name from a Gaulish goddess called Sequana and, at the spot where the river rises, a sanctuary dedicated to this goddess flourished between the 2nd or 1st century BCE and the first few centuries CE. Sequana's sacred springs became an important site for hopeful worshippers seeking healing and here archaeologists have unearthed roughly fifteen hundred *ex votos* – small votive offerings, often in the shape of human body parts. If a devotee wanted the goddess to cure a crippled hand, they might leave a wooden, metal or stone offering in the shape of a hand at the sanctuary. A petitioner suffering from liver or kidney problems might contribute an *ex voto* depicting the afflicted organ(s). Someone seeking a cure for sexual infertility might dedicate model genitalia. And so on.

Such anatomical offerings are a form of what is known today as 'sympathetic magic'. Sympathetic magic exploits sympathies or similarities between representational objects like the *ex votos* and their real-world equivalents (in this case, the worshippers' own bodies). If Sequana received a votive plaque with eyes carved on it, she would know that the worshipper wanted her to heal their eyes or improve their sight. The connection between such an *ex voto* and the desired result could also be more abstract: instead of asking the goddess for literal eyesight, the petitioner might be seeking insight or prophetic knowledge. This sort of magical logic still applies today when modern effigies or voodoo dolls are created, with the expectation that things done to the effigy will also occur to the person it represents.

Anatomical votive offerings like the ones found at the sanctuary of Sequana are still left at churches and shrines today around the

A wooden *ex voto* in the shape of a head from the Temple of Sequana at the source of the Seine.

world. In some Spanish-speaking Catholic communities today, for example, small charms called *milagros* are often placed in religious spaces, while in many Eastern Orthodox churches people offer similar objects called *tamata*. These are typically made from metal or wood and often depict body parts. The god(s) in question may have changed, but the thinking behind the ritual process is similar. Like people in the ancient world who left *ex votos* at the source of the Seine, most people who leave *milagros* or *tamata* at churches today probably do not think they are performing magic per se; they are simply engaging in an act of worship with the hope that it will impact their life and health in some positive way.

At the sanctuary of Sequana, people deposited a range of different items including coins, jewellery and a few inscriptions to the goddess, but the quantity and diversity of the *ex votos* are remarkable. Some of the most impressive of these are large wooden carvings of worshippers with life-size body parts, which have survived surprisingly well after nearly two thousand years thanks to the damp anaerobic (oxygen-free) soil conditions that prevented decay. One statue depicts a child holding a dog. The child in question might have been asking Sequana to heal a favourite pet or have brought the animal as a sacrifice to the goddess. Reading this today, most of us probably hope it was the former, and that the deity obliged.

A bronze statue of Sequana herself also survives from the sanctuary. The goddess is depicted as a woman wearing a crown and traditional Gallo-Roman clothing, standing in a boat. The prow of the boat is shaped like the head of a duck and the stern looks like a

An early trip to the vet at the source of the Seine? Limestone statuette of a child wearing a talisman and holding a dog.

The goddess Sequana and her majestic duck-boat, found at her sanctuary at the source of the Seine.

duck's tail feathers. The duck-boat imagery points to the goddess' association with water and the river. Her Gallo-Roman garments reveal the influence of Roman artistic styles and religious cults, reminding us that many gods were worshipped in multilingual and multicultural centres. This cult was not an exclusive club: anyone could ask Sequana for healing, whether Gaul or Roman, local resident or visiting pilgrim.

DAILY DEVOTION

Someone living in the western Roman Empire, whether they spoke a Celtic language or not, had a wide array of gods at their disposal in times of need. A soldier might dedicate an altar to Smertrios, Mars, Brigantia or Minerva. Someone with a broken leg or a chronic cough might honour Belenus, Apollo or Sirona. A person concerned about childbirth might make a pilgrimage to the source of the Seine to ask Sequana for help. Shoemakers in Spain sought out Lugus's assistance, while sailors in Paris proudly worshipped a number of gods together, from Cernunnos to Jove. Some of these gods and goddesses were clearly distinct entities, like Epona, and some were seen as facets of the same god, like Sucellus Silvanus. Some were worshipped locally, while others enjoyed widespread devotion. Although many of these gods were 'Celtic' in the sense that they have names that derived from Celtic languages or were venerated in areas where people spoke such languages, they were worshipped alongside other gods from the Greco-Roman world by people from multiple cultural backgrounds.

Snapshots survive of individual moments of devotion: the moment a group of boatmen erected a pillar; the moment a child carried their favourite pet to the sanctuary of Sequana; the moment a soldier from Syria thanked Epona under a strange sky far from home. These are valuable glimpses into the concerns and priorities of people living in the distant past but they show us only single instants in time rather than ritual processes. In the absence of any other evidence, it can be hard to speculate about how these deities were worshipped and what sorts of things people did to revere Taruos Trigaranus or Esus besides carving their names and images into blocks of stone.

Sometimes archaeological traces suggest how people worshipped in the past. The sanctuary of Sequana, located at the source of the Seine, was used and expanded over time, and we can make educated guesses from the archaeological record about the ways in which people moved through the series of rooms and pools in the sanctuary, bathing in healing waters and leaving offerings such as the *ex votos*, to the goddess whose aid they sought. We can also compare this evidence with what we know about healing cults elsewhere in the Greco-Roman world in places such as Aquae Sulis in Roman Britain (present-day Bath).

At Bath, the temple of Sulis Minerva was both a civic centre and religious space. Like many of the gods discussed above, Sulis Minerva was the result of syncretism between a local goddess named Sulis who was associated with nearby bodies of water and the Roman goddess Minerva. Some might choose to visit the shrine of another deity also worshipped at the site. A building has also been excavated at the site containing an image of the Roman moon goddess Luna; this might have been a temple space where people could spend the night and have their dreams interpreted by a priest the next morning. Then as now, dreams were important; they were believed to be visions from the divine or windows into a person's mental and physical wellbeing. By assigning meaning to these dreams, the priests could diagnose ailments and afflictions, and prescribe cures.

We also know that some of the priests who worked at or visited Bath were concerned with prophesying the future. An inscription on one stone from the site reveals that it was dedicated to the goddess by a *haruspex*. A *haruspex* was a special kind of priest in classical

Make your own *ex voto*

You will need: a piece of wood, clay or metal; a stylus, pen or other writing implement.

Instructions: Take a piece of wood or metal and draw or scratch a picture of a body part onto it using your stylus or writing utensil. Alternatively, carve a likeness of the body part from wood or mould one out of clay. This body part may be one you have recently injured (like a sprained or broken ankle) or it can represent something more abstract (e.g. if you want to get over a recent heartbreak, you may want to draw a heart). (Some creative licence is allowed for representing viscera.) Leave your *ex voto* for a god or goddess of your choice in a sacred space or carry it with you as a healing charm (in a pocket or handbag, or even hanging it round your neck is perfectly fine). If leaving it in a sacred space you should check with custodians of said chosen space to see if you are permitted to leave magical items there. Try not to leave your *ex voto* in nature unless it is 100 per cent biodegradable.

Modern *ex votos* made of wax from the Church of Our Lady of the Afflicted, Olhão, Portugal. Similar votive offerings can be found around the world.

Mars, depicted here in an early 16th-century engraving, was a favourite Roman god to syncretize with local deities, such as Nodens and Smertrios.

antiquity who foretold the omens based on the flight of birds or by looking at the entrails of sacrificed animals. These magical technologies were widespread throughout the Greco-Roman world and could be found in places inhabited by speakers of many different languages, Celtic or otherwise.

The bath complex at Aquae Sulis was a multi-activity centre. Visitors here (or at similar sites) could exercise in the *palaestra* (a changing area-cum-gym) before dipping into a series of baths of different temperatures: cold (*frigidarium*), mild (*tepidarium*) and hot (*caldarium*). In addition to providing a relaxing wash, the cleansing spring waters were thought to cure disease and illness. The baths also offered a chance to catch up with friends or chat to business partners: the Great Bath at Aquae Sulis was surrounded by niches where bathers could sit and play games, eat and drink, or simply enjoy breathing in the steam rising from the waters of the natural hot spring. Before departing, bathers would leave offerings for the goddess in the sacred spring – including many Roman coins that have since been recovered by archaeologists. Just as people today throw coins into wishing wells and fountains, so too the residents of and visitors to Bath threw their pocket change into the spring, hoping to secure some supernatural protection. People also placed in the spring personal prayers or petitions to the goddess written on lead sheets. Often these petitions sought divine retribution on behalf of their authors, as we will see next.

2

CURSE TABLETS

Roman Britain, 4th or 5th century CE.

Silvianus charged out of the temple of Nodens blinking and irate. He had gone to sleep in the temple precinct for the night, hoping the priests of Nodens would be able to interpret his recurring bad dreams and suggest a cure for his bad leg and now his favourite gold ring with its engraving of Venus was gone. And he knew who was to blame: that scoundrel Senicianus! Silvianus knew that revenge was required – Nodens wouldn't stand for this theft in his sacred precincts and the god was going to make Senicianus and all of his family pay for what they had done! Indignant and spouting maledictions, Silvianus bustled off to get a thin sheet of lead and a stylus, with which to pen his grievance.

Some distance away in the town of Calleva Atrebatum, Senicianus brought his newly acquired ring to an engraver's shop. He didn't want anyone to doubt it was his property so he was going to have his name inscribed on it. And that of his new god. Venus could stay on the bezel of the ring but Senicianus only worshipped the Christian God and He was going to protect his devotee. Senicianus laughed at the thought that Silvianus might ask his ineffectual pagan deities for retribution. Senicianus was beyond their power now.

This is a fictionalized account of the actual loss and attempted recovery of a ring in 4th- or 5th-century CE Roman Britain. We know about it from a curse written on a thin sheet of lead that was found at the site of a Romano-British temple dedicated to the god Nodens at Lydney Park in Gloucestershire. This sort of curse is known as a *defixio*, Latin for 'binding'. The idea is that a *defixio* magically binds or fastens the target of the curse or the supernatural powers enacting the curse to the will of the author in order to produce their desired outcome. The thin sheet of metal on which the curse was written is known as a *lamella*. The inscription on the Lydney Park curse tablet, written in Latin, reads: *To the god Nodens: Silvianus has lost his ring and given half [the value of the ring] to Nodens. Among those who are called Senicianus do not allow health until he brings it back to the temple of Nodens.*

Silvianus's *defixio* is a typical curse inscription from the Greco-Roman world: it asks a deity to help recover lost property and avenge the author upon a suspected thief and promises a reward to the god. What is unusual in this case is that archaeologists might have found the stolen ring that it mentions. In 1785, a gold ring was unearthed in the ruins of Calleva Atrebatum, a Romano-British town near modern Silchester in Hampshire, about 112 kilometres (70 miles) away from the temple of Nodens at Lydney Park. (The ring is currently held by The Vyne, a National Trust property located a few miles away from where the ring was found.) Engraved on the square bezel is the name Venus and the image of a face in profile, probably representing the goddess. Inscribed in Latin along the band of the ring are the words 'Senicianus, may you live in God'.

Senicianus's (stolen?) ring, *c.* 350–450 CE, lost for over a millennium and now in The Vyne, National Trust.

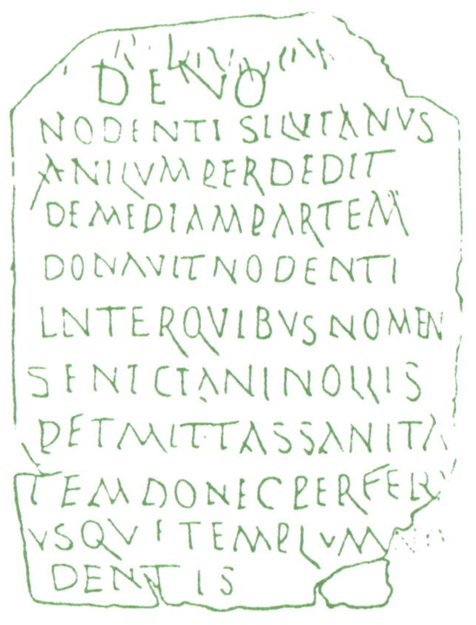

Drawing of Silvianus's curse tablet by archaeologist Mortimer Wheeler, who excavated the temple of Nodens at Lydney Park along with his wife Tessa Verney Wheeler.

While the inscriptions on both the curse tablet and the ring are in Latin, the name of the god invoked, Nodens, is Celtic. Versions of this name survive in the later Irish and Welsh languages, so it is likely Nodens was known in some form over a larger Celtic-speaking geographic area. The fact that Silvianus asks Nodens to withhold good health from Senicianus until the ring is returned echoes the god's probable associations with medicine and healing. The temple of Nodens at Lydney Park might have been a local healing centre, reflecting a hybrid Romano-British cult. The deity may have been Celtic in origin, but at Lydney Park he was worshipped with all the trappings of a traditional Roman temple, including a bathhouse and mosaic with classical Roman sea-creature designs. Inscriptions link Nodens with the Roman god Mars, indicating that they were syncretized like many of the Celtic and Roman gods discussed earlier. Several small figurines in the shape of dogs were also found at the site and were probably associated with Nodens in some capacity.

Perhaps they were considered to be sacred to him in the same way that horses were connected to Epona or peacocks were sacred to the Greek goddess Hera (Juno to the Romans).

Although the dramatic version of events given above is based on archaeological evidence, it is still ultimately fiction. We do not know if Silvianus was at the temple in search of healing, although it seems like a reasonable guess. Or that he lost the ring while asleep there. We can't even be sure that the ring found near Silchester was actually the same one that Senicianus had stolen from Silvianus, although the coincidence is striking. There are several other instances of the name Senicianus from Roman Britain (including in one of the Bath curses discussed below) so it may simply have been a common name. These other Seniciani might have been entirely separate individuals or members of the same extended family, although we cannot discount the possibility that one of them was a prolific thief, stealing small items across Roman Britain.

The ancient scene of the crime. Excavations at Lydney Park, *c.* 1920.

Likewise, while it has been suggested that the Senicianus whose name appears on the ring was an early British Christian, this is speculation. The formula 'May X live in God' is typical of early Christian inscriptions, but it is possible that it was merely intended to mean 'a god' rather than 'the Christian God' in particular. Either way, it invoked the protection of some deity in this world and perhaps the next. In addition, the very end of the inscription is incomplete because the last letter runs into the bezel of the ring – was it supposed to say 'may Senicianus live in (a) god' (perhaps the Christian God) or 'may Senicianus live in (a) goddess' (i.e. Venus)? It is possible that this represents poor planning and space allowance on the part of whoever engraved the words. Alternatively, the engraving of Venus

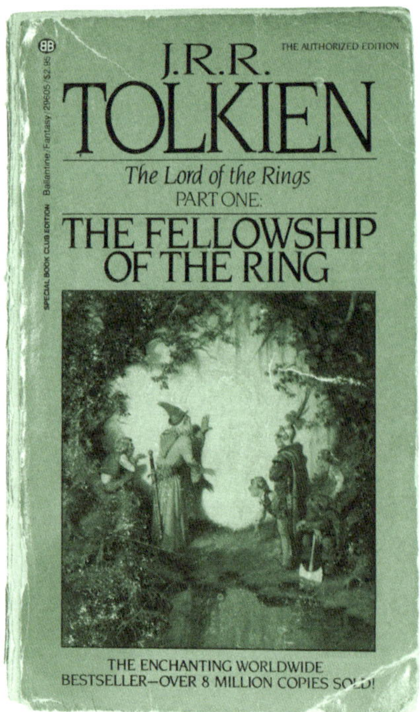

One ring to rule them all? The story of Silvianus's stolen ring may have inspired J. R. R. Tolkien's *The Lord of the Rings*.

on the bezel may have been added at a later date, covering up the end of the inscription on the band. In this case, perhaps a Christian artefact (if indeed it was a Christian artefact) was repurposed to feature a Greco-Roman goddess rather than vice versa, as suggested in the dramatized account above.

Nevertheless, even with some uncertainties, the *defixio* and the stolen ring make for a good story, and one that illuminates many features of daily magic in Roman Britain and other parts of the Roman world where speakers of Celtic languages and cults of Celtic gods were present alongside their Greco-Roman counterparts. Silvianus's curse and the case of the stolen ring might also have helped shape magic in modern fantasy fiction: Mortimer Wheeler, an archaeologist excavating the temple of Nodens at Lydney Park in the 1920s, consulted Oxford professor J. R. R. Tolkien on the meaning of the name Nodens in the Lydney Park *defixio* – leading some to suggest that it may have inspired the One Ring in Tolkien's *The Lord of the Rings*.

HOW TO CURSE YOUR ENEMIES: THE BATH CURSE TABLETS

The Lydney Park *defixio* is hardly unique in its content or style, however. Other similar, well-known curse tablets from Roman Britain were found in 1979–1980 at the Roman baths at Bath, Somerset. While bath complexes can be found across the Roman world, Bath (called Aquae Sulis by the Romans) is the location of the only natural hot spring in Britain and was a particularly important healing cult site in ancient times. Here, archaeologists discovered a group of 130 curse tablets in a sacred spring dedicated to the Roman-British goddess Sulis Minerva. Like the curse tablet from Lydney Park, the Bath *defixiones* consist of short inscriptions written on lead *lamellae*.

Bronze head of the goddess Sulis Minerva from a temple at the Roman baths in Bath, perhaps keeping a divine eye on would-be pickpockets.

The Bath *defixiones*, like the curse tablet from Lydney Park, consist of short inscriptions written not only in Latin but also (in the case of two tablets) in a Celtic language. Across the Greco-Roman world, Latin *defixiones* (in Greek they are called *katadesmoi*) were left in shrines, tombs and sacred places with the expectation that a deity (especially one associated with water or the Underworld) would enact the curse as requested. The range of offences that incurred curses was wide and varied. Someone may have created a *defixio* with the aim of regaining stolen property, as Silvianus did, or to win a legal case, avenge a wrongdoing, or defeat political, romantic, or even athletic opponents. *Defixiones* could be kept secret; a *defixio* concealed inside a tomb, for example, was unlikely to be publicly accessible. However, others were produced or placed in public spaces such as temples or baths, probably in an attempt to apply an element of social pressure as well as supernatural agency. If the offender got wind that they had been mentioned in a *defixio* they might take steps to avoid both divine punishment *and* public humiliation through proper redress and compensation.

Some *defixiones* were written directly by the person who was doing the cursing, while others were the work of professional scribes or magicians and can be very formulaic. Someone might consult a professional if their own ability to read and write was limited or if they believed the professional had special occult expertise that was more likely to produce the desired result. Both the Latin and Celtic inscriptions from Bath were probably the work of amateur individuals rather than practised scribes or magicians, as the handwriting is varied and spelling mistakes abound.

If the target of the curse was not explicitly identified in the inscription, many *defixiones* would call upon the deity to pursue the offender 'whether man or woman, whether enslaved or free, whether boy or girl'. You might have chosen to phrase your curse this way if you did not know who was responsible for a theft or if you were a professional scribe and your client had not provided you with a list of suspects. One *defixio* from Bath even specifies 'whether pagan or Christian' in the hope that the goddess invoked had power over adherents of multiple faiths, including Christianity. A curse might also include the promise of a reward to the deity whose aid had been requested. If theft was involved, the reward was often the value of the lost property, as promised in this Latin *defixio* from Bath:

> To the goddess Sulis I have given six little silver coins which I lost. Demanding [them] from the names written below is up to the goddess: Senicianus and Saturninus and Anniola.

Defixiones survive in Celtic languages as well as in Latin, Greek and numerous other languages of the ancient Mediterranean world. Curse tablets were produced in multicultural, multilingual societies and reveal the influence of Greco-Roman traditions alongside local customs. A *defixio* might be written in Latin but appeal to a Celtic deity (like Silvianus's *defixio,* which asks Nodens for help). Alternatively, it might be written in a Celtic language but mention individuals with Roman names. *Defixiones* could be encoded with letters written in reverse or with magical names or nonsense words, much like saying 'Abracadabra' today. Most people who produced or commissioned *defixiones* probably did not think they were engaging in specifically 'Celtic' or 'Roman' magic; they were simply trying to influence the world around them in one of the many ways they knew how. Indeed, *defixiones* were not necessarily the only way for someone to address a specific problem or situation. An individual who created or commissioned a *defixio* that was intended to impair their opponents' performance in court, for example, likely also hired legal counsel for good measure.

Unfortunately, it is more difficult to understand inscriptions in ancient Celtic languages than those in Greek or Latin. This is both because inscriptions are often fragmentary and because our knowledge of ancient Celtic languages is imperfect. Often we can be reasonably certain as to what genre an inscription belongs (calendars, curses, grave markers, etc.) and we can identify certain words or phrases, but scholars may disagree about how to interpret and translate a longer text. Bath Tabella 18 makes a good example of these sorts of interpretive problems. This is one of the two Celtic-language tablets so far identified from Bath (the rest are in Latin). It was clearly deposited in the sacred spring in the hope that Sulis Minerva would grant the petitioner's request. Experts are divided as to its interpretation, not least because it still isn't clear in what language it is actually written. The language is definitely Celtic because it shares important linguistic features with other Celtic languages, but beyond that it is unclear

A modern artist's impression of a day at the baths. Roman baths were usually segregated by gender.

Steam still rises from the geothermal waters
of the Great Bath today.

whether it represents an early survival of British Celtic (the language that would eventually become Welsh, Cornish and Breton) spoken by local Britons from the region or whether it is actually Gaulish as spoken by visitors from across the English Channel. Roman Bath was a busy place, visited by people from other parts of the empire, so this tablet easily could have been the work of a Gaulish tourist, trader, or soldier stationed nearby. Because we currently lack many other examples of the British Celtic language from the period (beyond a few names on coins), we do not have any good evidence with which to compare the Bath inscriptions. For now, therefore, the language of these two Bath inscriptions remains a mystery.

BATH TABELLA 18

The inscription on Bath Tabella 18 in the original Celtic language has been transcribed as follows:

Side 1:
adixoui

Side 2:
deịạna [or, *deuina*]
deịeda [or, *deueda*]
andagin
uindiorix
cuamịịn
ạị

Three proposed translations suggest the range of possible readings:

1. *I have dedicated a bath(?)/ointment(?) to the divine D.; (I) Vindiorix for the sake of (my) Sweetheart.*
2. *I, Vindiorix, O divine Deieda/Deveda, shall fix an evil (?fate [or similar]) on Cuamiina.*
3. *The affixed: Devina, Deieda, Andagin (and) Vindiorix I have bound.*

A significant range! It is not even clear whether Tabella 18 is in fact a curse or whether it is a dedication to the goddess in honour of a loved one, although the context in which the tablet was found suggests that it is likely to be a curse, since most of the longer Latin inscriptions from the same location are *defixiones*. The text probably has something to do with 'fixing' or 'binding' one or more offenders in order to secure vengeance or compensation, much as a *defixio* literally 'binds' or 'fixes' someone or something. One thing scholars do agree upon, however, is that Vindiorix is a name meaning something like 'white king' or 'fair king'. This does not mean the individual in the inscription was actually royal though, just as many people today are named Regina, Ryan, Rani, or Leroy, all of which come from the same root meaning 'king' or 'queen'.

The vast majority of the Latin *defixiones* from Bath are related to petty theft of items such as clothing or small amounts of money, so it would not be surprising if Bath Tabella 18 also targets a suspected thief and names one or more culprits. Since visitors to the sanctuary removed clothing and personal possessions before bathing, opportunities for theft on site were rife, although people might have asked Sulis Minerva to help recover items stolen elsewhere, in addition to those swiped at the baths.

Unusually for a curse tablet, Bath Tabella 18 is inscribed on a pendant that might have been worn before (or after) the curse was written.

GAULISH CURSES AT CHAMALIÈRES

The Bath inscriptions are relatively short, but longer *defixiones* survive from the ancient region of Gaul. One of these is a lead curse tablet from the springs at Source des Roches near Chamalières, Puy-de-Dôme département, Auvergne-Rhône-Alpes in France, where it was found alongside thousands of wooden anatomical *ex votos* like the ones mentioned in the previous chapter – unlike the fragmentary Celtic *defixiones* from Bath, this inscription is complete and in reasonably good condition. Just like the temple of Nodens Mars at Lydney Park and the sanctuary of Sulis Minerva at Bath, the springs at Source des Roches were a place where petitioners could seek both healing and divine retribution.

In the Chamalières inscription, which is written in Gaulish, the petitioner invokes the powers of the *andedíon diíiuion*, probably referring to 'Underworld gods', and specifically *Mapon Aruerriiatin* (the god Mapon/Maponos), possibly 'of the Averni people'. Since the Gaulish-speaking Averni lived in what is now Auvergne, the region in which Chamalières is located, this seems like a plausible translation. The name Maponos also appears in inscriptions from Britain and elsewhere in Gaul, so this Maponos 'of the Averni' might have been a local version of a more widely worshipped god. He appears to be either one of the group of 'Underworld gods' or at least a deity who was not incompatible with infernal powers. The Chamalières *defixio* may also mention the god Lugos in the closing section. The inscription repeats: *luge dessummíis* three times, which may mean something like 'serving Lugos'. Or it may mean something completely different: one scholar has suggested we read it as 'I prepare them [presumably, the offenders] for committing [to the god's vengeance]'. Once again, ancient Celtic inscriptions prove challenging to translate! The Chamalières inscription asks Maponos to be quick and probably to 'bind' a list of individuals who may have upset the author of the *defixio*.

The inscription also explicitly mentions *brixtía*, or 'magic', a word that is found in several other *defixiones* (including a tablet from Larzac in southern France, which we'll see shortly). Here, in the Chamalières tablet, the magic seems to be described as 'infernal magic' or the 'magic of the infernal ones', probably associating it with the Underworld forces at work. 'Underworld' or 'infernal' places and powers in this context do not necessarily carry the same negative connotations that 'hell' may for people today. It may simply refer to deities associated with underground or low-lying places (like the spring) or with a neutral Underworld – but it is still sinister enough in the context of a curse.

Since many such lead tablets with inscriptions found at springs throughout the Greco-Roman and Celtic-speaking world are *defixiones*, this would suggest that we should indeed read the tablet as a curse. One scholar, however, has suggested that the Chamalières inscription may actually be an innocent healing prayer rather than a malevolent *defixio*. Many *ex voto* models of body parts were also found nearby, evidence that people came to the springs seeking cures. Moreover, the inscription seems to mention ailments including crookedness and blindness, although rather than medical conditions in need of healing these may be physical punishments that the author is asking Maponos and the infernal gods to inflict upon their enemies. To add to the difficulty of interpretation, in several inscriptions from Roman Britain, Maponos is invoked as 'Maponos Apollo', a syncretized deity combining Maponos and the Greco-Roman god Apollo, who was often associated with healing in the ancient Mediterranean world. Although the Chamalières inscription does not mention Apollo, it is possible that Maponos had similar local associations at Source des Roches.

In the case of both the Bath and Chamalières *defixiones*, the act of depositing the curse in the sacred spring was just as important as the words written on the tablets. Unfortunately, in the absence of a handy instruction manual supplied with the tablets, we can only speculate as to what other components the cursing ritual might have

At 4 x 6 cm (1⅗ x 2⅖ inches), the Chamalières *defixio* is slightly smaller than a credit card or driving licence.

involved. Did the petitioner draft their *defixio* on a wax tablet or a scrap of papyrus or parchment first and then copy it onto the lead *lamella*? Did they read their curse out loud or recite other magic words as they threw it in the spring? Was the *defixio* thrown into the spring under cover of night or did the petitioner display it somewhere prominently first, giving the offender a heads-up as to what was in store? If the *defixio* was commissioned from a professional scribe or magician, how much did it cost? Did the petitioner make a gift to the deity's shrine before or after creating the *defixio*, or only if the *defixio* had proved effective?

Just as the language and content of *defixiones* vary, the rituals by which curses were created and enacted likely varied from place to place and person to person as well. The text of the Chamalières inscription is rhythmical, as is the inscription on the Larzac tablet (discussed next), so both of these could have been read like poetry or chanted aloud, suggesting an oral ritual component not unlike a magic spell. In a multilingual part of Roman Gaul or Britain, the choice to write a *defixio* in a Celtic language rather than in Latin probably reflected the petitioner's own cultural background and relationship to the gods. Perhaps some people thought that curses worked better

Gallo-Roman *ex votos* from Source des Roches, found near the Chamalières curse tablet.

Like many of the *ex votos* at the Temple of Sequana at the source of the Seine, those from Source des Roches are made of wood and depict various body parts, especially heads.

in their native tongue. Or perhaps certain gods were more likely to respond to a curse in a particular language. Although if a professional was commissioned to produce a *defixio*, the language of the inscription was probably dependent on the scribe or magician who wrote it.

WOMEN AND MAGIC AT LARZAC

The late 1970s and early 1980s were a good time to be excavating Celtic curse tablets. In addition to the Bath and Chamalières tablets found around this time, the longest-known inscription written in Gaulish was unearthed in 1983 at the La Vayssière necropolis near L'Hospitalet-du-Larzac, Aveyron département, Occitanie in southern France. The Larzac inscription is also a *defixio* and names multiple women and at least one man. Unlike the *defixiones* from sacred springs, the Larzac tablet was found in a tomb, dating to the late 1st century or early 2nd century CE, which probably belonged to a woman called Gemma (the name 'Gemma' appears on a large vase found within the tomb). The *defixio* was discovered on top of a funerary urn, positioned like a lid, presumably placed there shortly after Gemma's death and before the tomb was sealed in the hope that the petition would accompany Gemma's spirit to the Underworld and be delivered to the proper deity. It is unclear whether Gemma herself had anything to do with the *defixio* (if indeed she was actually the occupant of the tomb) but since Gemma was probably already dead when the *defixio* was written and since her name appears nowhere in the inscription as it survives today, it seems unlikely that she was its author or its target. It is much more likely that the author(s) of the *defixio* were opportunistic acquaintances or relatives who wanted Gemma's soul to conduct their message to the infernal powers. Her spirit became a sort of supernatural carrier pigeon, delivering the curse to its intended recipients.

The Larzac tablet, like the other *defixiones* discussed so far, is difficult to read today for a number of reasons. It survives in two fragments and some of the text is missing, mostly from the end of the inscription. The inscription as we have it is the work of two scribes – the second scribe deleted parts of the first scribe's text. On top of this, we also have all the usual problems with reading an ancient language that is not well attested and with which we do not have much other material to compare directly. Once again, we must accept that we do not fully understand what the text says, although we can identify some elements and make educated guesses.

Firstly, it looks like the Larzac inscription invokes a goddess named Adsagsona. Unfortunately, we don't know much more about Adsagsona as her name does not survive in any other known inscriptions. Her name may be related to a root word that has something to do with 'seeking' (justice?) and she was presumably considered a deity who could enact the justice or vengeance required from the curse. Continuing to piece together the *defixio*, the first lines of the

The Larzac *defixio* survives in two fragments; it might have been broken intentionally by its author(s), or it might simply have become damaged with time.

The names on the Larzac Tablet

The following women are mentioned in the Larzac inscription:

Bano[na] Flatucias •
Paulla dona Potiti[us]
Aiia • duxtir • Adieg(i)as
Poti[ta m]atir Paullias •
Seuera du[xtir] Valentos dona Paullius
Adiega • matir • Aiias
Potita dona Primius Abesias [...]
Rufena Casta dona [Ba]non(i)us [...]
C Vlationicnom
Aucticnim [m]aterem Potiti(as)
Vlatucia mat[ir] Banonias

We can (tentatively) translate this as:

Banona [daughter?] of Flatucia [probably a spelling variation for the Vlatucia below]
Paulla dona of Potitia
Aiia daughter of Adieg(i)a
Potita mother of Paullia
Severa daughter of Valens, dona of Paullia
Adiega mother of Aiia
Potita dona of Primia [daughter?] of Abesia...
Rufena Casta dona of [Ba]non(i)us...
Caius Vlationicnos
Aucticnia mother of Potitia
Vlatucia mother of Banonia

inscription also mention *bnanom brictom* or 'magic of women', just as the Chamalières inscription mentioned *brixtía* 'magic'. So far, so good. But then things get tricky.

Shortly after the mention of Adsagsona another name appears: Severa Tertionicna. Severa is a standard first name for a Roman woman and Tertionicna is a Gaulish patronymic indicating that she was related to a man named Tertiu or Tertius. So, she belonged to a mixed Gaulish and Latin society, which is in keeping with the Greco-Roman style of the *defixio* and what we know about Roman settlement in Gaul. The opening of the inscription mentions a *uidlua*, which probably means 'seer' or 'woman who knows things' and may describe Severa Tertionicna herself as a possessor of prophetic or magical knowledge.

A list of many more names appears later in the inscription, linked by words identifying their relationships, such as 'Aiia daughter of Adiega'. The words 'daughter' and 'mother' appear frequently, providing clues about family or social relationships between these individuals. If they formed part of a group of magicians or coven of witches, perhaps the relationships in question were figurative rather than familial: older members of the group might have sponsored or mentored younger women in the group. Another word used to link the women in this inscription is *dona*, such as 'Paulla *dona* of Potitia'. This word is more opaque. It clearly also refers to a type of relationship – suggestions include 'lady', 'foster-mother', 'foster-daughter', 'nurse' or 'heir' – but is left untranslated here. Among the names, just two are male: Caius Vlationicnos and Valens. The individual Caius Vlationicnos is named in his own right rather than appearing as part of a patronymic, while the name Valens is probably only mentioned to clarify that the Severa in this part of the inscription is his relation and not the Severa Tertionicna (the relative of Tertiu/Tertius) mentioned earlier. Many of these names and the grammatical forms used show a mix of Latin and Gaulish, indicating that the community to which these individuals belonged was multicultural and, to some degree, multilingual.

In addition to Severa Tertionicna, this gives us a list of about ten women, along with the two men, at least one of whom is merely included as the relative of one of the women and does not seem to be involved in his own right. But who is doing the cursing and who is being cursed in this *defixio*? Are the women listed here the same individuals whose 'magic of women' is described at the beginning of the inscription? And what do they have to do with Severa Tertionicna?

Some ideas proposed include:

1. The group of named women are followers of Severa Tertionicna and they are all being cursed by the author(s) of the *defixio*.
2. The group of named women are followers of Severa Tertionicna and they are all cursing someone else.
3. Severa Tertionicna is cursing the group of women.
4. The group of women is cursing Severa Tertionicna.

Severa Tertionicna and/or the group of women might have persecuted each other or the unknown author(s) of the *defixio* in the past, or be about to do so. The two scribes who wrote the *defixio* may have created the curse or may have simply been commissioned to inscribe it. Like the other *defixiones* we have seen, certain words in the Larzac inscription appear to refer to the Underworld and to the action of 'binding'. This type of magic was reasonably common. The wording of the tablet (in so far as we can work it out) looks similar to other (more intelligible) *defixiones* in Greek and Latin from throughout the ancient Mediterranean, and it was found in a necropolis that shows the influence of Roman burial practices. In this particular case, some elements of the curse recall the sorts of phrasing and lists of names found in Greek and Latin judicial prayers and curses. It has been suggested that the Larzac tablet is a judicial curse, meant to influence the outcome of a court case, or a counter-spell intended to keep supernatural forces at bay (such as the 'magic of women', which presumably posed a risk of disruption in the case of legal proceedings).

Nearly two thousand years after the Larzac *defixio* was written, we may not understand all the details of the inscription, but we

Gallo-Roman *terra sigillata* vessel from La Graufesenque, a site where other Gaulish inscriptions have also been found, such as administrative accounts from local potteries.

can name a group of women (and one or two men) who lived in a small town in Roman Gaul. These were probably not very wealthy people nor significant political actors who would have made much of a mark on the historical record otherwise, but we know their names, nonetheless. We know that these women had a complicated network of relationships that extended well beyond the men in their families. They performed magic or were seen as formidable enough opponents that magic was used against them. Thanks to one fragmentary curse tablet, we can still hear a rare echo of their ancient voices and spells.

The people involved in the production of the Larzac tablet experienced very real conflicts and they were prepared to go to the length of putting a curse tablet into a freshly made tomb and invoke the powers of the Underworld in order to solve them. This was a serious business and we should not take their magical efforts lightly. A strong desire

Make your own *defixio*

Need some inspiration for your everyday imprecations? Choose one of the following examples of ancient curses, according to your grievance. Write your curse on a thin sheet of metal or wood (or a pen and paper will do the job). Fold your *defixio* and bury or deposit it in a sacred site. Alternatively, you can post it somewhere prominent to attract the attention of the offender(s).

To recover lost property (based on a Latin *defixio* from Uley, Britain):

> *[Your name] to the sacred god Mercury. I bewail to your divine power: I have lost [stolen item(s)]. I would ask the spirit of your divine power that you do not permit health to the one who has engaged in theft against me nor let them lie down, sit, drink, or chew, whether man or woman, boy or girl, enslaved or free, until they have brought my item back to me....*

To punish deceit (based on a Latin *defixio* from Gallia Narbonensis in southern France):

> *Just as this lead [tablet] is not visible and disappears, so may the lifetime, limbs, life, livestock, grain, and goods of those who evilly engaged in deception against me also vanish: [list names of offenders here].*

To win a legal case (based on a Latin *defixio* from Bregenz, Austria):

> *[Names of opponents]: the adversaries of [your name or the name of your associates] and whoever speaks against [you or your associates], destroy all of them. I ask you to give all those who plan evil for [your name or the name of your associates]... to give to Ogmios to be taken away by death.*

for retribution or a pressing fear of magical harm drove people to produce these *defixiones*. We can only wonder whether they achieved their purpose.

While such behaviour may appear extreme to us today, it is not uncommon to find *defixiones* buried in or near graves in the Greco-Roman world, and many more may be waiting to be uncovered.

To prevent someone from marrying (based on another Latin *defixio* from Bregenz, Austria):

> *Ogmios will give to the spirits the health, heart, ankles, kidney, anus, genitals, ears, little basket, utensils of [the target of the defixio]: they will obey him [i.e. Ogmios], so that [target of defixio] cannot marry, by the anger of the god.*

To get even with your enemies (based on a Latin *defixio* from Trier, Germany):

> *[Name of offender(s)]: I ask you, Lady Isis, to invoke the bleeding (or, diarrhoea) on [the offender]. May whatever [name of offender] has that is good fall into terrible disease.*

You can substitute the deities listed here with one or more of your choice:

Celtic gods: Sulis Minerva, Nodens, Maponos, Adsagsona, Ogmios

Greco-Roman gods: Mercury, Neptune, Jupiter, Juno, Mars, Diana, Castor and Pollux

Other gods: Isis (an Egyptian goddess), Mithras (an Iranian god popular with soldiers)

Anonymous gods: infernal powers, underworld ghosts, water nymphs

Note: while people in the past often cast their *defixiones* into sacred springs, Sulis Minerva does not take kindly to pollution and so we do not advise throwing your *defixio* into modern bodies of water. The effectiveness of any of the above *defixiones* is entirely the responsibility of the petitioner. As is the effect of any counter curse, for which we also cannot be held liable.

In early 2025, French archaeologists announced the discovery of over twenty new curse tablets from a necropolis near Orléans, Loiret département, Centre-Val de Loire, at least one of which is written in Gaulish. The inscriptions remain to be studied in depth but hopefully they will reveal new insights into the Gaulish language and the practice of ancient magic.

3

GREEK AND ROMAN IDEAS ABOUT CELTIC MAGIC

Gaul, 1st century BCE.

All the nation of Gaul is dedicated completely to religious practices. Because of this, those who are afflicted by grave diseases and who take part in battles and dangers either sacrifice humans as victims or dedicate them to be sacrificed, using the druids as ministers to these sacrifices, for it is thought that unless the life of a person is given for the life of (another) person, it is not possible for the power of the immortal gods to be appeased. Others have figures of great size woven from twigs, the limbs of which are filled with living people. When they are set on fire, the people are killed surrounded by flames. It is thought that the sacrifice of those who had been caught committing theft or robbery or other crimes is more acceptable to the immortal gods. However, when abundance of this sort is scarce, they even sink to sacrificing the innocent.

JULIUS CAESAR, *GALLIC WARS*, BOOK 6.16

CAESAR AND THE GAULS

In his military memoirs, written during the 1st century BCE, Julius Caesar presents us with a dramatic and disturbing scene in which the ancient Gaulish priesthood of druids burns people and animals alive inside a giant wicker statue. The gods of the druids that Caesar describes are bloodthirsty beings that can only be appeased by human

A sensationalized 18th-century illustration based on Caesar's equally sensational account of 'wicker man' sacrifices.

sacrifice. While criminals are the usual choice of sacrifice, even innocents can face the flames when the gods demand.

Over the last two thousand years this gruesome image has inspired numerous writers, scholars, artists and cult-horror filmmakers. Yet there is no indication that Caesar or any of the other Latin and Greek writers who also described such Gaulish 'wicker man' sacrifices had ever actually seen one take place. This doesn't mean that something like it didn't happen but we should be sceptical of indirect sources written by people who belonged to other cultures and who were often subject to their own biases. However, some of these classical Greek and Latin accounts about ancient Celtic ritual predate the written evidence about magic in Gaul and Britain that we have already seen and, if handled with care, might provide more detailed clues about what Celtic speakers believed and how they practised their beliefs. These Greco-Roman accounts are not free from error or prejudice and they can be difficult to evaluate. For this reason, I have chosen to save this classical evidence for last, after encountering ancient Celtic speakers in their own words in the first two chapters.

Julius Caesar's account comes from his *Gallic Wars*, a book written to justify his ongoing conquest of Gaul to Romans at home, some of whom were becoming concerned about Caesar's growing military strength. This concern turned out to be well-founded, as Caesar later marched on Rome with his legions, starting a civil war that lasted for four years and ended with him assuming dictatorial powers before ultimately being assassinated. Caesar had multiple aims in writing *Gallic Wars* and it is an oversimplification to call it merely a work of propaganda but, among other things, it was intended to convince Caesar's Roman audience that his prolonged campaign in Gaul was both politically and morally necessary. One of the ways in which he managed this was to present the Gauls as a group of barbaric people whose continued autonomy presented a threat to Roman security and an affront to good moral sensibilities. Caesar does not come

A 17th-century engraving of Gaius Julius Caesar (100–44 BCE). The Roman general turned dictator is an important (but not always reliable) source for the inhabitants of ancient Gaul.

straight out and say this in so many words: instead, he writes about himself in the third person, creating a facade of objectivity behind which he could conceal his own motivations.

Partway through Book 6 of *Gallic Wars*, Caesar digresses from his earlier cut-and-dry military account and describes the culture and religion of the Gauls and the Germans. It is debatable whether these observations are intended to reflect Gauls and Germans in their entirety, or only particular groups of them. It is also unclear whether we should take 'Gaul' to mean someone who speaks Gaulish or someone who lives in the vaguely delineated region called Gaul, and likewise whether 'German' refers to someone who speaks a Germanic language or to someone who lives in the area known as

Germania at the time. Perhaps the biggest problem here for modern scholars and people interested in ancient Celtic societies is the fact that Caesar does not claim to have witnessed personally any of the rites or practices he describes, nor does he mention any eyewitness sources or native interlocutors. In fact, he does not provide any direct evidence to back up his claims whatsoever.

Anyone who tries to dehumanize their enemies strategically is unlikely to be an accurate source for information about said enemies and we should take anything Caesar says with several grains of salt (possibly an entire shaker). While ancient writers did not always have the same ideas about proof and evidence that historians do today, we should be wary of any text that does not at least attempt to list its sources or analyse the origins and credibility of the material it recounts. With these problems firmly in mind, what can we actually learn from Caesar about the Gauls and magic (if anything)?

Caesar tells us that the Gauls worship Mercury as their chief god, followed by Apollo, Minerva, Mars and Jupiter. This reference to the Roman pantheon to explain Gaulish gods is in keeping with the examples of syncretism between Gaulish and Roman deities seen in the previous two chapters. It is possible that, at the time Caesar

Coin minted by Caesar c. 48–47 BCE showing the goddess Venus on one side, and the shield and carnyx (a type of long horn) of conquered Gaul on the other.

was writing, several Gaulish gods were already fused with Roman or Greek deities, but syncretism certainly became far more pronounced after Gaul became a Roman province. Caesar's approach in explaining Gaulish gods as manifestations of loosely similar, but far more familiar, Roman gods might instead have been exclusively for the benefit of a home crowd that knew little about Gaulish religion. Indeed, he goes on to list the spheres of patronage associated with each god: Apollo repels illness, Minerva looks after crafts, Jupiter rules the heavens, and Mars is associated with war. Caesar also reports that the Gauls believe that they are descended from Dis, the Roman god of the Underworld, and that as a result they count the passage of time by nights instead of days.

According to Caesar, Gaulish druids train for as long as twenty years and often travel to Britain to do so, as this is supposedly where druidic arts originated. As we will see in the second part of this book, medieval Celtic languages spoken in Britain and Ireland have inherited words for 'druid' and it would make sense that a loosely similar priesthood existed in multiple Celtic-speaking areas at the time Caesar was writing. Yet apart from Caesar's report, we have no way of knowing how long druids-in-training spent learning their profession or whether the practice originated in Britain. It is slightly suspect that Caesar, who had been unsuccessful at invading Britain in 55 and 54 BCE, identified that particular place as the source of a bloodthirsty and barbaric priesthood, but his account may still contain some element of truth.

Some of Caesar's other claims about Gaulish religion can be at least partly substantiated with other sorts of evidence. For example, he writes that the Gauls dedicate to Mars any items captured in battle: they burn animals and leave piles of captured weapons in sacred places. Romans themselves dedicated captured enemy spoils to their gods, so some elements of this account might have reflected Roman practices familiar to Caesar. In this case, however, modern archaeology has supported some of Caesar's claims. At Gaulish sanctuaries at Gournay-sur-Aronde, Oise département and Ribemont-sur-Ancre, Somme département, France, human and animal bones and broken weapons have been found in enclosure ditches around a central shrine. The campaigns that Caesar describes in Book 6 of *Gallic Wars* took him near both sites, so it is entirely possible that he did observe ritual practices firsthand or spoke to people who had witnessed such rituals themselves. While we should not accept all of Caesar's information about Gaulish religion uncritically without other evidence, sometimes it appears that he was correct. Comparable accounts of Gaulish practices by other ancient writers including the historian Diodorus Siculus and the geographer Strabo also exist – perhaps they observed similar evidence themselves, or perhaps they drew on a source that was known to Caesar as well, or even used Caesar himself as the source.

Caesar also says that the druids discourage committing sacred information to writing for fear that it will ruin people's memories, although other Gauls use Greek letters to record everyday information – and we do have evidence of Gaulish written in the Greek alphabet in inscriptions from southern Gaul near Greek trading colonies. We do not have early written evidence for Gaulish religious or magical texts but it is unclear whether this is due to druidic decree (as Caesar says), loss of evidence over time or whether long texts in Gaulish were simply not written down before the 1st century CE.

Caesar clearly had his own agenda when writing about his Gaulish enemies but, unlike some of the other ancient authors who wrote about the Gauls, Caesar had at least been to Gaul, knew a number of Gauls personally and was acquainted with at least one druid. This was Diviciacus (sometimes spelled Divitiacus), a leader and diplomat of the Aedui group of Gauls who travelled to Rome to ask for Roman help to defend his people against neighbouring groups. This 'help' eventually took the form of Caesar's continued conquest of Gaul. We know from the Roman writer Cicero that in addition

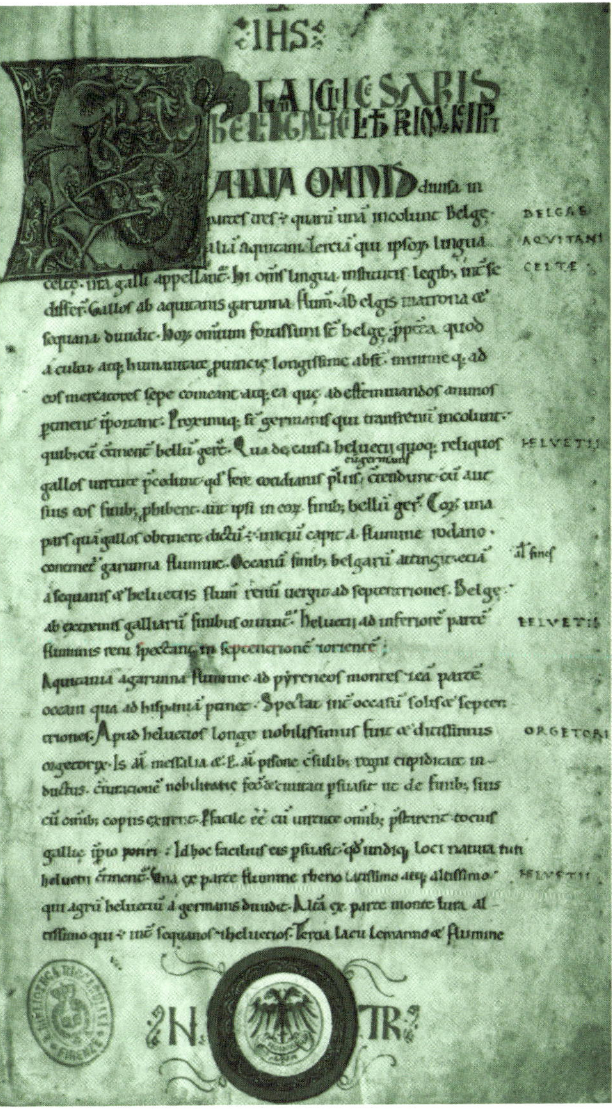

An attractive medieval copy of Caesar's *Gallic Wars*.

Lucan on the Gaulish bards and druids

The Latin poet Lucan, who wrote in the middle of the 1st century CE (about a century after Caesar's death), had some of his own ideas about Caesar's enemies. Here, in his epic poem *Pharsalia*, he describes a resurgence of wild Gaulish rites after Caesar and his legions withdrew from Gaul to fight in the Roman Civil War. Lucan was a poet and wrote with considerable creative licence (as poets are want to do), so he probably isn't the most accurate source on Gaulish religion from a century beforehand. (A 'bard' is a type of poet. The terms 'Erebus' and 'Dis' describe the Underworld.)

You bards also, who, as prophets to distant ages, recall
the strong spirits cut off in war with praise,
poured forth your many songs securely.
And druids, putting down your weapons, you reclaimed
your barbaric rites and sinister custom of worship.
To you alone it is given to know (or not to know)
the gods and celestial powers. You inhabit the distant groves
in remote forests. You teach that shades
do not descend to the silent throne of Erebus and the pale
kingdom of Dis below, but the same spirit governs its limbs
in another world: if what they say is believed, then death is merely
the middle of long life. Thus the peoples on whom the pole star gazes
are happy in their error, since the greatest fear,
the fear of death, does not oppress them. Thence the mind
of the warrior is inclined to rush into arms, and their spirits
are ready for death: it is cowardice to spare a life that will be renewed.

to being a Gaulish statesman, Diviciacus was a druid. If Cicero was correct, this makes Diviciacus the only druid from antiquity whose name we know from contemporary sources.

Cicero himself was friends with Diviciacus and hosted him in Rome. The writer specifies that Diviciacus was a druid in a work he wrote about predicting the future called *De Divinatione* ('On Divination').

Cicero tells us that Diviciacus 'professed that the understanding of nature which the Greeks call physiology was known to him and he used to speak about things which would come to pass, partly through augury and partly through inference'. 'Physiology' here should be understood in its ancient sense as 'natural science' broadly construed rather than as the modern medical discipline. In Cicero's account, Diviciacus comes across as a philosopher who is well-acquainted with the natural world. He makes predictions about the future through deduction or through augury, a method of foretelling the future that in the Roman world typically involved observing the movements of birds. From this description, Diviciacus sounds more like a Greek intellectual or a Roman priest than a barbarous, bloodthirsty Gaul. Cicero's text is ultimately an argument against all types of divination but he spends as much time discrediting Greco-Roman beliefs as foreign ones and Diviciacus comes off no worse than his Roman contemporaries.

Caesar generally portrays Diviciacus in a favourable light and notably does not call him a druid. Perhaps this is because Caesar had painted a negative portrait of druids and did not want to admit that his chief Gaulish ally, who had given him an excuse to pursue his invasion licitly, was in fact a druid. Diviciacus might have been the source of some of Caesar's information about druids as he was for Cicero. If Diviciacus was Caesar's main font of knowledge for Gaulish customs and beliefs, this might be another point in favour of Caesar's reliability as a source on Gaulish religion. However, even if a Gaulish source like Diviciacus stands behind Caesar's account, we still cannot tell what Caesar might have changed or added for his own political purposes. Caesar also appears to have relied on an established body of information about the Gauls and their religion known to other Greek and Roman authors and ascribed to the Greek writer Posidonius.

POSIDONIUS AND THE PROBLEM OF SOURCES

Most scholars accept that much of what Caesar says about Gaulish culture and religion is in fact drawn (directly or indirectly) from an earlier Greek philosopher named Posidonius. Posidonius wrote during the 2nd and 1st centuries BCE and was considered in ancient times to be an expert on many topics. His writings only survive today, however, in quotations preserved by later authors. Posidonius's ethnography (a genre of writing about usually foreign peoples) of the Gauls influenced Caesar, as well as the ancient Greek authors Strabo and Diodorus Siculus, among others, who in turn influenced still later writers. This is to say that most ethnography about the ancient inhabitants of Gaul comes down to us today via a circuitous, millennia-long game of Telephone. Perhaps Posidonius himself had witnessed the

Bust of the Greek philosopher Posidonius (c. 135–51 BCE), now in the Naples Archaeological Museum.

rituals he describes during his travels around the Mediterranean or heard about them from other travellers, but it is just as possible that he too drew on a now-lost source text or that he simply made up some (or all) of his observations from scratch.

Scholars today tend to refer to this frequently repeated muddle of information about the Gauls as the 'Posidonian tradition'. However, since Posidonius's own writings do not survive, they cannot be assessed independently from their use by later authors who quote his work. Nor is it always clear whether later authors drew their information directly from Posidonius, a source misidentified as Posidonius, or other intermediary authors who claimed to be quoting Posidonius. This does not mean that Posidonius and his literary heirs contain completely fabricated information about the Gauls, but it does mean that it is difficult (if not impossible) to confirm what they tell us. When later writers made use of Posidonian traditions, we must wonder whether they were merely copying and pasting from an older text or whether they had observed any of the details themselves.

Based on the testimony of later writers, a core set of shared details about Gaulish religion emerges, although these details are not always represented identically. Classical authors generally agree, however, that druids predicted the future (possibly the least controversial claim), dedicated the spoils of battle in sacred places (which seems to be archaeologically attested, as discussed earlier), practised human sacrifice for various ends, and preached a doctrine of reincarnation.

Human sacrifice is one of the most salaciously and frequently reported aspects of Gaulish religion in accounts from antiquity. Caesar writes about the infamous 'wicker man' sacrifice in which people were burned alive inside giant wicker structures. Strabo gives his own version:

> [I]t is said that there are other forms of human sacrifice: for they shoot some (victims) with arrows, and impale some in sacred places, and having built a giant of hay and wood

> and thrown in livestock and all kinds of wild animals and humans, they burn it as an offering.

Human sacrifice was not unknown in the ancient Mediterranean world and it might very well have taken place in Gaul and Britain too. However, in cases where we have archaeological evidence of violent death, it is difficult to tell whether such injury was due to criminal execution, sacrifice, murder, death in battle, or some combination of the above. For example, bog bodies found in Britain and Ireland show clear evidence of violent death and were probably ritually killed. Without further (ideally, written) evidence, therefore, it is hard to say whether the people whose bodies were preserved in bogs died through religiously motivated sacrifice, judicial execution, murder or a mixture of all of the above. The bodies of ancient people who died by violence have been found in bogs throughout Europe. They are not unique to Celtic speaking places nor do classical authors like Caesar mention that Gaulish human sacrifices took place specifically in or near bogs or marshy areas, so we are probably dealing with a wider ancient phenomenon rather than a specifically Celtic one.

If Caesar is to be believed that criminals were executed as sacrifices in Gaul, this would not necessarily be obvious from any physical remains that survive today. Caesar, Diodorus Siculus, Strabo and the Greek writer Athenaeus are alike in claiming that the Gauls burn their sacrificial victims, and Diodorus Siculus echoes Caesar's and Strabo's elaborate descriptions about burning human and animal sacrifices, which may ultimately owe their source to Posidonius. While Caesar and Strabo assert that this fiery end takes place in a wicker figure, Diodorus Siculus describes a simpler pyre. Diodorus Siculus and Strabo also describe a gruesome divination ritual by which the Gauls stab prisoners and try to divine the future from their death spasms and the patterns of their blood. Pomponius Mela and the Roman poet Lucan prefer to leave the sacrificial details vague.

Strabo (c. 64/63 BCE–24 CE) is represented here as a medieval gentleman in the *Nuremberg Chronicle* from 1493.

Another oft-repeated feature of Gaulish religion that can probably be traced to Posidonius is the claim that the Gauls believe in reincarnation. Most Romans believed that their souls went to the Underworld after they died but there were plenty of ideas circulating in the ancient world about what happened after death. Some, like the Greek philosopher Pythagoras and those who followed his teachings, believed in reincarnation. Caesar, Diodorus Siculus, Strabo, Ammianus Marcellinus, Pomponius Mela, the poet Lucan and others attribute belief in reincarnation to the Gauls but present it in slightly different ways. Caesar and Pomponius Mela offer cynical interpretations, suggesting that the druids promoted belief in reincarnation so that Gaulish warriors would not be afraid to die in battle—the idea being that if they believed that another life awaited them after death, perhaps they would fight even harder in this one. Diodorus Siculus connects Gaulish beliefs in reincarnation directly to Pythagoras, perhaps because fusing elements of Gaulish belief with a philosophy familiar in the ancient Mediterranean world would make things more comprehensible for his readers. Yet, despite these ancient assertions, we do not know if Celtic speakers in antiquity actually believed in reincarnation or not. Even if some of them did, beliefs probably varied by individual and location.

THE ROMANS AND FOREIGN MAGIC

For all the religious syncretism discussed so far, the Romans were often inherently suspicious of foreign magic and foreign cults. According to the 1st-century CE historian Suetonius, the first Roman emperor Augustus forbade druids from becoming Roman citizens, while the

Bronze head of the emperor Augustus (63 BCE–14 CE), found at Meroë, Sudan.

Cameo of the emperor Claudius (10 BCE–54 CE) depicted as the Roman god Jupiter. Note Jupiter's characteristic eagle companion on the left.

successive emperors Tiberius and Claudius prohibited the religion of the Gaulish druids outright. In the words of Suetonius, Claudius banned the 'dreadful cruelty' of druidic religion.

This sort of religious animosity usually had political rationale and was not confined to Gaulish beliefs. As early as the 2nd century BCE, the Roman Senate severely limited the worship of the Greco-Roman god of wine Bacchus (the Roman version of the Greek god Dionysus). Roman citizens and allies who were caught celebrating the Bacchanalia could be punished with death. The target of imperial bans on druids was not necessarily Gaulish religion itself (as we have seen, many Gaulish gods and cult sites continued to flourish under Roman rule) but rather higher-status druids who might have marshalled anti-Roman sentiment among the Gaulish elites.

The Romans also had plenty of pre-existing prejudices against the Gauls. In addition to Caesar's need to justify his conquest, Roman authors and audiences would have connected the contemporary inhabitants of Gaul with the Gaulish sack of Rome under Brennus in about 387 BCE. By Caesar's time in the 1st century BCE this had become something of a legendary event in Roman historiography. After the incorporation of Gaul and later Britain into Roman territory under Caesar and his successors, Celtic-speaking and Latin-speaking societies clearly merged to some extent, but literary and ethnographic tropes about the Gauls and Britons and their supposedly barbarous ways continued to linger in the minds of later ancient authors.

ANCIENT MAGICAL CONVENTIONS

In addition to problems with the reliability of ancient Greek and Roman accounts discussed so far, including propagandist motives and uncertain sources, Greek and Roman authors were also liable to draw on a common set of magical tropes and stereotypes found around the ancient Mediterranean world. It should be clear by now that Celtic speakers often practised religion and magic in ways that were very similar to their Greco-Roman neighbours. Like many other people in the ancient Mediterranean and Near East, Celtic speakers relied on curse tablets as a way of controlling or punishing adversaries. They left *ex votos* at healing sites and they often worshipped deities who had been syncretized with Greek or Roman gods. It should not surprise us, therefore, that Greek and Roman authors often describe Celtic speakers practising magical arts that are akin to what the Greeks and Romans did themselves. However, in the absence of other evidence, some of the ritual behaviours in Greek and Roman accounts of Celtic speakers look suspiciously similar to magical conventions found in Greco-Roman culture....

For example, the Roman naturalist and historian Pliny the Elder recounts an elaborate ritual in which Gaulish druids dressed all in

Druids gather mistletoe under the moon in a painting by Henri-Paul Motte, *c.* 1900. Pliny's account of druids gathering mistletoe on the fifth day after the new moon has provided inspiration for numerous later writers and artists.

Pliny the Elder peruses a book of exciting and improbable creatures, from an engraving, 1584.

white cut sacred mistletoe from oak trees with golden sickles on special nights. According to Pliny, the druids catch the mistletoe in a white cloak as it falls from the tree. They proceed to sacrifice two white bulls and hold a great feast. The mistletoe is brewed into a potion that, when drunk, increases fertility and provides protection against poisons. This is a picturesque scene of magic, which has proved popular with modern illustrators and artists, but does it contain any truth?

It is striking that a similar scene appears in Virgil's *Aeneid* when Queen Dido of Carthage performs a series of mock rituals, ostensibly to get her lover Aeneas back after he has left her, but in actuality to prepare for her own suicide:

> She sprinkled liquids representing the springs of the underworld,

and herbs were sought under the moon, harvested with
bronze sickles,
flourishing with black poisonous sap.

Dido attributes these rituals to a mysterious priestess from the far west. The herbs gathered at night with a sickle made of a special metal look rather like Pliny's druids cutting mistletoe by moonlight. Was Virgil drawing on established conventions of ancient magic, perhaps also practised by the druids? Or did Pliny model his druidic rituals on literary tropes like those in Virgil's work? Or both? Similarly,

In one of the most famous scenes from Virgil's epic, Dido kills herself after Aeneas has deserted her, from an engraving, *c.* 1520.

when Pliny says that druids wear white robes, does this reflect the clothing of real druids, or is Pliny merely importing his own expectations based on what plenty of other priesthoods in the ancient Mediterranean world wore?

Pliny is plainly dismissive of the magic beliefs of other (non-Roman) peoples. After describing the druidic mistletoe ritual, he quips 'such is the religious devotion to frivolous things of many peoples'. A little later, he also comments:

> Gaul also possessed magic up through living memory. For the reign of Tiberius abolished their druids and those types of prophets and physicians. But why do I mention this art which has also crossed the ocean and reached the empty space of nature? Today thunderstruck Britain worships with such rites that it might seem that Britain gave [magic] to the Persians. People across the whole world are similar in this way, although they are separate and ignorant of one another. It is not possible to value sufficiently what is owed to the Romans who abolished these terrors....

For Pliny, many non-Roman populations practised magic in much the same way and were alike in their dedication to superstitious nonsense. His Roman audience could thank their own rulers for abolishing such silly and sometimes violent practices throughout the empire. Pliny lumps the magic of Gaul and Britain together with magic in the rest of the world and clearly did not think highly of any of it. We may question whether he was in fact the most discerning or reliable source for such ritual practices. While people in the ancient world and the Middle Ages rarely drew a clear distinction between religion and magic, in a way Pliny's division between foreign magical arts and proper Roman religion mirrors modern-day divides between organized religions practised

Waves lash and lightning flashes over this fabulously anachronistic impression of 'Vercingetorix and the druidess', *c.* 1880.

The ancient Greek enchantress Medea stalks the halls with a flask of poison in Evelyn de Morgan's 1889 painting.

centrally and everyday magic performed independently. Indeed, this starts to look something like the rhetoric of early modern and modern imperialism, which often placed local and non-European magical practices at the bottom of an artificial hierarchy of religions in an effort to justify conquest and colonial rule.

Another classical trope may be reflected in accounts of priestesses on islands near Gaul and Britain. Strabo quotes a now-lost account by Posidonius, claiming that priestesses of Dionysus live on an island in the mouth of the River Loire. Men are not allowed on the island, although the women sometimes leave in order to have sex with men and then return. Once a year, a violent sacrifice takes place: the women replace the roof on their temple and if one of them drops their load of roofing material, she is torn to pieces by the others in a mad frenzy. As they tear her apart, the frenzied women cry 'Euhoi'. (The reader is assured that someone is always jostled so that she drops her load and the sacrifice can occur.) Those who know their ancient Greek tragedy may recognize the ritualistic roar of *euhoi* from works like Euripides's play *The Bacchae*, in which wild worshippers of Dionysus rend people apart in a possessed outburst. We must wonder whether Posidonius's anecdote, via Strabo, reveals more about the Greco-Roman literary conventions than it does about ancient Celtic ritual practices.

Celtic-speaking priestesses on islands also feature in a work by Pomponius Mela, who tells us that nine virgin priestesses dedicated to a Gaulish deity reside on an island named Sena in the sea opposite Brittany (this is probably somewhere between Brittany and Cornwall and may be one of the Scilly Isles). These women are said to have magical powers: they can stir up storms, shapeshift into animals and cure incurable diseases. They are great prophets and can reveal the future to anyone who travels to their island.

So, we already have two accounts of groups of magical women living on islands: the unnamed island near the Loire and the island of Sena (possibly just off Cornwall). Another Roman writer, the historian Tacitus, also makes similar comments about sacred women and islands existing among the inhabitants of Germania. To what degree were all these accounts about supernatural women and islands simply creative invention or the result of literary motifs passed on from writer to writer, and to what degree did they represent reality? Should we envision real priestesses conjuring storms and tearing apart sacrificial victims, or are these once again classical attempts to portray the barbarism and exoticism of people living on the periphery of the Mediterranean world? Weather magic and shapeshifting are powers commonly attributed to witches in classical mythology, such as Circe or Medea, so perhaps once again, like Pliny's white robes and mistletoe, classical writers also turned to their own familiar cultural institutions to represent unfamiliar foreign priesthoods.

The Greco-Roman god Apollo was associated with prophecy and divine healing across the ancient world. Here, the god is depicted in a statue from the Temple of Apollo, Cyrene, Libya, 2nd century CE. In Gaul, Apollo became syncretized with the god Belenus.

The druids of Anglesey

The Roman historian Tacitus writing in the late 1st and early 2nd century CE paints a striking picture of the Roman conquest of Mona (present day Ynys Môn/Anglesey in northern Wales):

> *The hostile battle line stood on the shore, dense with weapons and men. Women ran in between like Furies in funeral clothing with dishevelled hair and carried torches. And all around the druids, pouring out dire prayers to heaven with raised hands, terrified the [Roman] soldiers with the strangeness of this sight so that as if with limbs stuck fast and unmoving they exposed their bodies to wounds. Then from the exhortations of their leaders and one another's urging not to fear a frantic army of women, they carried their standards forward and scattered the opposition and enveloped them in fire. Afterwards a guard was put over the vanquished and the groves which had been dedicated to savage superstitious were destroyed: for [the druids] thought it was proper to honour altars with the blood of captives and consult the gods with the viscera of humans.*

ANCIENT MAGIC: A LONG SPELL?

The rest of this book will focus on magic in medieval Britain and Ireland, but before we leave ancient Gaul, we must ask: how much longer did ancient magic persist? In the 4th century CE a Latin writer and teacher named Ausonius, from what is now Bordeaux, France, wrote a poem praising the ancestry of a friend:

> You are sprung from the line of the druids of the Baiocassi [inhabitants of modern Bayeux, France], if rumour does not deceive belief, and draw your sacred descent from the temple of Belenus, and the names of your family come from there: you are Paterae; thus the mystics call the ministers of Apollo. The name of your brother and father is given from Phoebus and your child from Delphi.

How to communicate with the dead

According to the ancient writer Diodorus Siculus, Gauls wrote letters to recently deceased kin and at their funerals cast these letters upon the pyre in the hope that the departed would be able to read them in another life. (This may be an exaggeration on the part of Diodorus Siculus but it is not entirely out of keeping with the placement of curse tablets in tombs in both Gaul and throughout the ancient Mediterranean world.)

Funerals are liminal times and tombs liminal spaces between the worlds of the living and the dead, so it makes sense that they presented ancient worshippers with opportunities to speak to souls beyond the pyre or the grave.

You can try your own letter-burning ritual to share your thoughts and news with a deceased friend or relative. In the absence of a flaming funeral pyre, a match or lighter will suffice, but please use responsibly.

An early 19th-century druidical costume design.

If earlier writers are to be believed about Roman imperial attempts to suppress the druids in the 1st century CE, there weren't many druids floating around in Bayeux in the 4th century. Ausonius makes an educated allusion to the druids of former times rather than suggesting that his friend's family were still practising druids. Ausonius syncretizes the Gaulish god Belenus with the Greco-Roman deity Apollo (who was also called Phoebus and whose oracle was located in Greece at Delphi), just as we saw in inscriptions in Chapter 1, so he was evidently still familiar with some combination of temple dedications, regional traditions and written accounts about Gaulish and Roman gods in the area. It is possible that Apollo Belenus was still being worshipped locally, but as the 4th century progressed, Christianity became increasingly widespread throughout the Roman world to the eventual exclusion of polytheism.

Another roughly 4th-century CE text called the *Historia Augusta* also mentions several episodes involving female druids who foretell the rise and fall of the Roman emperors Alexander Severus and Diocletian and prophesy the success of the emperor Aurelian's descendants. These events are set in the 3rd century CE but they probably reflect dramatic conventions rather than historical reality. If these *Historia Augusta* episodes do contain any kernel of historical truth (or at least truth as it was perceived in the 4th century CE), these women would be the only explicitly female druids mentioned in the entirety of our ancient accounts. Some Gaulish religious officiants were probably women (and as we saw earlier, women in Roman Gaul certainly practised magic, such as those listed on the Larzac tablet), but we have no other unambiguous evidence for female druids in antiquity from classical or archaeological sources.

Finally, before we move on to medieval magic, we have time for one more, very late archaeological attestation of druids from outside the Roman world. A 5th-century inscription from Ireland includes the word *DRVVIDES*. It is unclear whether the word in the inscription is in Latin or Irish, although in either case the presence of any kind of writing in Ireland reflects contact with literate cultures across the Irish Sea during a period of trade, conversion to Christianity and political instability after the Romans departed from Britain. It is also uncertain whether the inscription refers to druids as we have come to know them from our ancient Greco-Roman sources, as they appear in later medieval literature, or whether they were envisioned in an entirely different way altogether. Unfortunately, the inscription is very brief and doesn't tell us much more but it is a tantalizing clue to the sorts of religious and cultural changes occurring in Celtic-speaking areas and on the edge of the Roman world at the end of antiquity as Christianity spread across Europe, bringing with it literacy to places such as Ireland, which had never formed part of the Roman Empire. It is to Britain and Ireland that we will turn for the remainder of the book.

PART II

MEDIEVAL MAGIC

4

PROTECTIVE PRAYERS AND SAINTLY AID

The Hill of Tara, Ireland, 5th century CE.

The druid Lucet Máel's rage was almost palpable as the veins on his head stood out in anger. His attempts to poison the saint had failed. His fellow druid had been smashed against a rock by the saint's strange power. Now the saint had cleared the fog and snow that he had conjured up to test his power, as easily as if he was blowing away the smoke from a recently extinguished torch. One more test would suffice to show whose god ruled Ireland. And it would involve more smoke than a mere torch.

A house-shaped structure was built on the plain before Tara, one half constructed of green wood and one of dry twigs. Patrick blessed his youngest disciple, Benignus, and wrapped him in the druid's cloak. The boy walked fearlessly into the dry part of the house. The druid pulled Patrick's shirt over his head and stomped angrily into the green part of the structure. The entire house was set on fire. Patrick moved his lips in silent prayer.

When the smoke finally cleared, Benignus was unscathed and sat calmly covered in the ashes of what had once been the druid's cloak. On the other side of the house nothing was left of the druid besides a heap of cinders, but Patrick's shirt shone bright, cleaner than ever. The people cheered and Patrick praised God.

This story is based on the *Life of St Patrick*, written in the 7th century CE by the Irish monk Muirchú. Both Muirchú and his contemporary

Tírechán, who also produced a biography of St Patrick, were working at a remove of at least two centuries from the events that they portray. Their depictions of pre-Christian Irish society are as biased and shaped by concerns of their own time as those of the ancient Greco-Roman writers we have seen. We cannot turn to these works for accurate information about religious beliefs and magical practices in pre-Christian Ireland, but we can explore what a monastic author in the 7th century *thought* about magic, druids and the process of conversion. Here, we will delve into several kinds of what might be termed 'magic' in medieval Celtic-speaking regions. These include

St Patrick in a stained-glass window from St Benin's Church, County Galway, Ireland.

the spells of wicked magicians, miracles worked by medieval saints and protective prayers that everyday medieval people used to defeat the powers of evil.

Fundamentally, during the Middle Ages, 'magic' was inseparable from 'faith'. Just as people in the ancient world believed that magic was simply a part of the natural world, for many people in the Middle Ages, magical, miraculous, or supernatural events were all part of the divine plan. Medieval magic was a continuum: at one end were magicians like the druid Lucet Máel, who practised the dark arts, often with the aid of demons; at the other end were saints like Patrick, who defeated evil and whose spiritual aid could be invoked through prayers. The ritual actions of normal people fell somewhere in the middle. They might pray for saintly help with formulaic protective prayers, recite medical charms over broken bones, or take other ritual precautions to keep evil forces at bay. Crucially, however, for medieval Christians, God was ultimately the source of all power, natural or supernatural. It was God who allowed saints to perform miracles, listened to the prayers of worshippers and sometimes even permitted demons or magicians like Lucet Máel to work sorcery so that saints like Patrick could triumph over them.

SAINTS VS MAGICIANS

Some of the earliest surviving medieval Irish sources that mention magic come from the earliest surviving narratives of the conversion of Ireland: namely, Latin accounts of the lives of saints known as 'hagiographies' (the word comes from Greek and means 'holy writing'). Two of these early hagiographies about St Patrick, Muirchú's *Life of St Patrick* and Tírechán's *Collectanea* ('Collected Stories'), share a number of the same episodes and probably drew from similar source material, if not also from one another. In both accounts, Patrick overcomes

St Patrick lights the Easter flame at the Hill of Slane, leading to a standoff with King Lóegaire and his druids.

antagonistic magicians, either by violence or conversion, in order to bring the Word of God to the Irish people. In these Latin texts, the magicians in question are referred to as *magi* (singular *magus*). The same word is used for pagan magicians in the Old Testament and to refer to the Three Wise Men who visit the infant Christ in the Latin Bible, and is the ancestor of the words 'magic' and 'magician' in English. Scholars have identified these *magi* in the early *Lives of St Patrick* as druids based on their role in the text and in later hagiographies in both Latin and Irish. Indeed, one of the first surviving attestations of the vernacular Irish word *druí* ('druid') appears as a gloss on *magus* in an 8th- or 9th-century manuscript. In a slightly later, 10th-century, Irish poem the three *magi* who attend Christ's birth are called druids. Both Tírechán and Muirchú draw heavily on Biblical models. Patrick becomes both Christian Apostle to the Irish and Old Testament prophet, while the druids with whom he contends take on the guise of evil *magi* like those in the Old Testament or like St Peter's adversary Simon Magus (Simon the *Magus*) in Acts of the Apostles.

The central conversion narrative of Muirchú's *Life of St Patrick*, set on the Hill of Tara, occurs on Easter Sunday when Patrick vanquishes

King Lóegaire's druids through miraculous means, leading the king to convert to Christianity. The king has been holding a pagan feast while Patrick has been trying to celebrate the eve of Easter by lighting the Paschal fire. Lóegaire and his druids take this as a sign that Patrick's religion will overwhelm them if the fire is not extinguished at once. Lóegaire tries to kill Patrick and God retaliates by dropping one of the king's druids from a great height, killing the druid (this is the same way that the Biblical wizard Simon Magus was said to have perished). Things settle down briefly but the next morning, on Easter itself, one of Lóegaire's remaining druids, Lucet Máel, tries to poison Patrick, and when this fails he proposes a series of miracle contests between himself and the saint. These contests initially take the form of weather magic in which the druid causes snow and fog to appear and Patrick removes it. The contest culminates in a trial by fire.

Ideas about magic and magicians in medieval Europe were often influenced deeply by the Bible. The final contest between the druid

St Patrick's bell and its shrine. The bell dates to c. 500 CE, near the time of Patrick, while the shrine is a later medieval creation dating to c. 1100.

and Patrick in Muirchú's Life also bears striking resemblance to the 'trial of divinities' in the Book of Daniel in the Bible. In the Book of Daniel, King Nebuchadnezzar throws three youths into a furnace to be burned, while in Muirchú's Life, one of Patrick's companions is exposed to fire but, through God's grace, emerges miraculously unharmed. Muirchú makes this connection explicit, calling Tara the Babylon of the pre-Christian Irish and comparing King Lóegaire to the Biblical Nebuchadnezzar.

We find saints contending with evil magicians in plenty of other hagiography as well. These magicians are not exclusively male, nor are they necessarily presented as remnants of a pagan priesthood like the druids in Muirchú's *Life of St Patrick*. For instance, in an early Latin *Life of St Samson of Dol*, the Breton saint crosses paths with a wicked old woman who lives in the woods and can fly through the air. In the text, she is called a *theomacha*—literally, 'someone who fights against God'. Samson ultimately defeats her (of course).

The Lives of early saints usually present pagan magic-workers as largely negative forces that God's saints must overcome in order to establish Christianity in new regions and convert new populations. However, there is room to manoeuvre within even these early depictions and, as we will see, later vernacular Irish literature is often more ambiguous in its attitudes towards pre-Christian Irish paganism and magic.

WEATHER MAGIC

In medieval hagiography harmful weather magic was often associated with magicians and demons. In Muirchú's *Life of St Patrick*, for example, the saint and his antagonist, Lucet Máel, compete in a series of weather-related miracles: the druid brings damaging snow and fog through his magical incantations, which Patrick banishes

Druidic haircuts?

Lucet Máel burns to a crisp in Muirchú's *Life of St Patrick*, but Patrick has greater success in converting a number of other druids to Christianity, according to Tírechán's *Collectanea*. When they convert, we are told, these druids need a new hairstyle (actually a head shave) to show that they are no longer druids but now Christians. The style of haircut sported by druids is referred to as *airbacc giunnae* or a 'frontal curved tonsure' but we don't have much more detail about what this looked like. It seems to have involved a curved hairline across the front of the forehead or perhaps the top of the skull while the rest of the front of the head was probably shaved. Whether pre-Christian Irish druids really did have special haircuts is not known – since Tírechán presents them as a group of evil priests, perhaps it is not surprising that he also claims they have their own style of monastic yet villainous hair. Other medieval writers sometimes also claim that Irish druids inherited their tonsure from Simon Magus, the famous Biblical magician.

with God's aid. In this story, the druid only has the ability to work harmful magic; he lacks the power to remove the bad weather he has conjured up and only Patrick (through God) is able to disperse the fog and melt the snow. The druid's spells constitute a negative (and ultimately ineffective) parallel to Patrick's positive benedictions, which are closer to a particular type of protective prayers, or *loricae*, at which we will look later.

In Adomnán's late 7th-century *Life of St Columba*, the titular saint encounters a challenge from the *magus* Broichan (again, perhaps *magus* ought to be translated as druid) while travelling in Scotland. Broichan makes good on a threat to send darkness and wind to hinder Columba's travel upon Loch Ness, but the saint prays to God and, instead of hindering his progress across the lake, the turbulent weather is harnessed to aid his transit. Like Lucet Máel, and the *theomacha* in the *Life of Samson*, Broichan has some control over the air and winds, but his magical powers are no match for the saint and the will of God. Adomnán takes this moment to remind the reader that sometimes God permits *magi* to raise tempests through the aid of evil spirits. He provides the example of St Germanus, who once defeated a legion of demons that sought to prevent his missionary and preaching activities by attacking him upon the stormy sea. From a medieval Christian perspective, all power ultimately came from God and sometimes God allowed demons or magicians to exercise some occult powers precisely so that saints could vanquish them. Columba and Germanus, like Patrick, demonstrate their sanctity by calming the bad weather that pagan *magi* and demonic forces have caused.

Saints often work weather miracles even when they are not combatting demons. In one episode from an early Latin *Life of St Brigit*,

St Columba is best known for founding the monastery of Iona but according to Adomnán's *Life of St Columba*, he also banished the Loch Ness monster.

St Brigit (or Bride) catches a ride with the angels in John Duncan's 1913 painting *Saint Bride*.

the saint hangs her cloak on a sunbeam! The Welsh saints Cadog and David are both credited with miracles by their medieval hagiographers (a 'hagiographer' is someone who writes hagiography) in which books abandoned in the rain miraculously remain dry and undamaged. The preservation of books was a primary focus of concern for medieval authors (perhaps unsurprisingly) and we find several similar miracle stories in Adomnán's *Life of St Columba* in which books lost in rivers for several days survive unharmed. Indeed, later in the same account, we are told that books written by the saint's hand are so holy that if taken and read outside they can produce rain after a drought. In another miracle, the act of praying over Columba's books helps monks summon favourable winds for a sea journey.

MIRACLES, MAGIC AND RELICS

Besides Adomnán's *Life of St Columba,* we know from other sources that manuscripts said to have been written by the saint were held in high esteem. Columba was traditionally believed to be the scribe of a 6th-century psalter (a book containing the Psalms from the Bible) known as the *Cathach*. It is one of the earliest surviving manuscripts from Ireland and indeed one of the earliest surviving Latin psalters from medieval western Europe. *Cathach* translates as 'Battler'. The book got its name because the Ó Domhnaill family who owned it used to carry it into battle with them in order to invoke the saint's aid. From the late 11th century onwards, the *Cathach* was kept in a special bejewelled container called a *cumdach* or book shrine. The manuscript itself is now in the Royal Irish Academy, while the *cumdach* is in the National Museum of Ireland. While most manuscripts from early medieval Ireland have been lost, the status of the *Cathach* as a holy relic probably accounts for its survival to the present day.

Bejewelled *cumdach* built to keep the *Cathach* of St Columba safe. Christ is pictured in the centre with St Columba (left) and the Crucifixion (right).

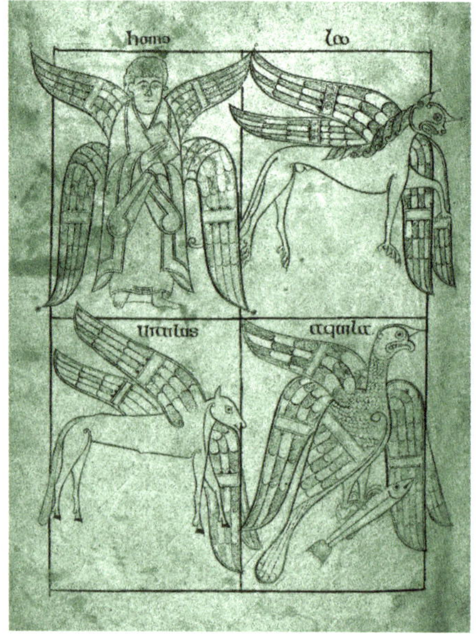

Illustration from the Book of Armagh showing the symbols of the four Evangelists (clockwise from top left): Matthew (human), Mark (lion), John (eagle) and Luke (calf).

A number of other medieval Irish manuscripts of the Psalms, Gospels, or parts of the Mass were kept in similar book shrines and reliquaries. One notable example, the Book of Armagh, was treated as a relic of St Patrick and kept at the saint's church in Armagh. It once was believed to have been partially written by Patrick himself. The manuscript dates from the 9th century CE, so we know today that it cannot have been the work of the saint, although it does contain copies of texts that Patrick authored.

Can we consider these book relics to be magic? Or indeed any of the myriad other physical reminders of saints, such as bells associated with saints like Patrick, Ruadán, or Cuileáin; the arm of St Lachtin; or the Cross of Cong that held a fragment of the True Cross upon which Christ was crucified? For many people in the past and still around the world today, relics possess power and grant miraculous connections to the holy figures they represent. Praying over relics or coming into physical contact with them was and still is a ritual action that brings some worshippers closer to the divine across multiple world religions. For a medieval Christian, visiting a holy relic in a particularly important church was akin to the ancient cure-seekers who sought divine revelation or physical healing at the springs of Sulis Minerva or at the Temple of Sequana. There are many religious differences between medieval Ireland and 1st-century Roman Bath, but on some level the desire to travel to a sacred place and interact with sacred objects in order to achieve a divine or supernatural connection is universal.

Two 12th-century Irish relic shrines containing a fragment of the True Cross (left) and the arm bone of St Lachtin (right).

ANGRY SAINTS AND HOLY CURSES

As we saw in the opening excerpt from Muirchú's *Life of St Patrick*, saints could be violent in pursuit of their holy goals. One episode from the Life of the Welsh St Cadog gives the denouement of the Indiana Jones film *Raiders of the Lost Ark* a run for its money when, after a miscreant violates St Cadog's Church in Llancarfan in Glamorgan, southern Wales and tries to plunder the community's wealth, he is literally melted: 'the sorry violator of that shrine melted away in the sight of the whole army, like wax in front of the fire'. Nor is Cadog the only Welsh saint who melts evildoers. When a nobleman cuts off the head of a girl named Wenefred who has refused to sleep with him, St Beuno also causes him to be melted

---

St Samson and the standing stone

An early medieval Latin *Life of St Samson of Dol* contains a story about pagans worshipping an idol near a standing stone in Cornwall. Throughout the Celtic-speaking world (and elsewhere), prehistoric standing stones were reused by later Christians to build churches and mark boundaries. These stones were often already associated with important sites in the landscape and they offered ways for new communities to create ritual continuity with the past (in addition to providing useful building materials for the present). Sometimes people carved crosses onto them, like Samson does in this story.

> *Now it came to pass, on a certain day, as he was on a journey through a certain district which they call Tricurius, he heard, on his left hand to be exact, men worshipping a certain idol after the custom of the Bacchantes, by means of a play in honour of an image. Thereupon he beckoned to his brothers that they should stand still and be silent while he himself, quietly descending from his chariot to the ground and standing upon his feet and observing those who worshipped the idol, saw in front of them, resting on the summit of a certain hill, an abominable image. On this hill I myself have been and have adored and with my hand have traced the sign of the cross which St Samson with his own hand carved by means of an iron*

---

like wax (Wenefred is then resurrected by Beuno and becomes a saint as well). Saints Teilo, Illtud and Congar also melt malefactors in their hagiographies.

Irish saints sometimes made their displeasure known by fasting against kings or secular powers that were obstructing them. In medieval literature, fasting against someone entailed refusing to eat until the demands of the person abstaining from food were met, much like a modern hunger strike. Fasting also demonstrated the ascetic virtues of the saint and their innate holiness. In one late medieval Breton play about the Life of St Non (the mother of St David), St Patrick makes an appearance and fasts against God, who has told him to leave Britain for Ireland.

---

instrument on a standing stone. When St Samson saw it, selecting two only of the brothers to be with him, he hastened quickly towards them, their chief, Guedianus, standing at their head, and gently admonished them that they ought not to forsake the one God who created all things and worship an idol. And when they pleaded as an excuse that it was not wrong to celebrate the mysteries of their progenitors in a play, some being furious, some mocking, but some of saner mind strongly urging him to go away, the power of God was made clearly manifest. For a certain boy, driving horses at full speed, fell from a swift horse to the ground and twisting his head as he fell headlong, remained just as he was flung, little else than a lifeless corpse. Then St Samson, speaking to the tribesmen as they wept around the body, said, 'You see that your image is not able to give aid to the dead man. But if you will promise that you will utterly destroy this idol and no longer adore it, I, with God's assistance, will bring the dead man to life.' And they consenting, he commanded them to withdraw a little further off, and, after praying earnestly over the lifeless man for two hours, he delivered him, who had been dead, alive and sound before them all. Seeing this, they all with one accord, along with the afore-mentioned chief, prostrated themselves at St Samson's feet and utterly destroyed the idol.

In a cluster of medieval Irish texts about St Ruadán, the saint protests against the Irish king Díarmait mac Cerbaill, who has abducted a man seeking sanctuary with Ruadán. Ruadán and another saint fast, ring bells and recite the psalms at the king until he complies with their wishes. St Ruadán tells Díarmait mac Cerbaill that his kingdom will fall and that none of his descendants will rule after him. This statement is somewhere between a prophecy and a curse – the king has upset God by violating the saint's sanctuary and events come to pass as the saint has predicted. The recitation of psalms, which often had benign or benedictory purposes, as examined below, could also expose wrongdoing and be used to punish an evildoer.

In another well-known medieval Irish text called *Buile Shuibhne* ('The Frenzy of Suibhne' or 'Sweeney Astray'), the titular Suibhne angers St Ronán and is punished for his actions. Suibhne steals a psalter from one of Ronán's clerics and throws it in a lake, whereupon an otter

A decorated crozier (a special staff carried by a bishop). This one was commissioned by Niall mac Meic Aeducain, bishop of Lismore in the early 12th century.

This 8th- or 9th-century chalice found at Ardagh, County Limerick was used for liturgical purposes. The names of the apostles are inscribed around the bowl.

returns it unharmed to the saint, much like the books miraculously saved from water damage in the *Life of St Columba*. This is not enough for Suibhne, who also kills the saint's foster-son and punctures the saint's bell with his spear in the process. At this point, Ronán is done with Suibhne's antics and curses him to die by spear point:

My curse on Suibhne!
Great is his guilt against me,
his smooth, vigorous
dart he thrust through my holy bell.
That bell which you have wounded
will send you among branches,
so that you shall be one with the birds –
the bell of saints before saints.
Even as in an instant went
the spear-shaft on high,
may you go, O Suibhne,

in madness, without respite!
You have slain my foster-child,
you have reddened your spear in him,
you shall have in return for it
that with a spear-point you shall die.

St Ronán turns Suibhne's own violence against him: just as Suibhne killed the saint's foster-son and destroyed the bell with his spear, so shall he die by a spear himself. Suibhne subsequently goes mad in battle and wanders the woods behaving like a bird for several years, which parallels the Biblical Nebuchadnezzar who, at one point in the Book of Daniel, loses his senses and lives as an animal for seven years. Suibhne finally dies when a swineherd kills him with a spear because he mistakenly believes that Suibhne is having an affair with his wife. Another saint, St Moling, appears to give Suibhne the last rites and promptly curses the swineherd for committing murder. Among the morals of the story is do not upset saints! This sort of saintly eye-for-an-eye vengeance is not all it seems at first, however, as Suibhne is eventually redeemed by his wanderings and St Moling blesses him before he dies.

LORICAE: PROTECTIVE PRAYERS

In addition to visiting holy sites and relics and enjoying miracle stories, another way that people living in medieval Ireland could engage with saints like Patrick and invoke their power and assistance was through reciting a type of protective prayer known as a *lorica* (plural *loricae*). While anyone could pray for St Patrick to intercede with God on their behalf at any time, a *lorica* was deemed to be particularly effective against evil. In Latin, the word *lorica* refers to a type of armour worn over the chest and upper body and it is often translated as 'breastplate' in the titles of medieval prayers. The regular recitation of these prayers was believed to provide the reciter with spiritual armour against the sorts of demonic forces that saints routinely defeated in their hagiographies. Like the ancient *defixiones* that literally 'bound' their victims, medieval *loricae* often use language of 'binding' – in this case, binding the worshippers themselves to Christ.

One of the best-known *loricae* from medieval Ireland is attributed to St Patrick. It is written in Old Irish, the form of the Irish language spoken between about 600 and 900 CE, which dates it to several centuries after the historical Patrick lived, so it was almost certainly not actually authored by the saint. Regardless of who wrote this *lorica*, however, it was intended to invoke St Patrick's powers of intercession and protection. In an 11th-century CE manuscript called the *Liber Hymnorum* ('Book of Hymns') the *lorica* appears, alongside many other prayers and homilies, with the title *Fáeth Fiada*. Subsequent medieval and modern readers alike interpreted this title as 'Deer's Cry' (possibly because there is a story about Patrick disguising his companions as deer in order to escape King Lóegaire in some of the medieval Lives of the saint). Scholars today, however, generally translate *fáeth fiada* (or *féth fiada*) as 'mist of a seer', a magical mist that appears in Irish literature to conceal Otherworldly characters from mortal sight. In the case of the *lorica*, this mist is miraculous – just as Patrick veiled his companions from Loégaire's wrath, so too can the person who recites the prayer veil themselves from evil powers.

St Patrick's *lorica* offers protection against the 'spells of women' (*brichta ban*). This phrase recalls the very similar phrase 'magic of women' (*bnanom brictom*) that appears in the ancient Gaulish curse tablet from Larzac, but does not necessarily demonstrate any close connection between the Irish *lorica* and the Gaulish *defixio*. The medieval author (or authors) of the Irish prayer wouldn't have known about the Larzac tablet – after all, the Larzac tablet was produced a thousand years beforehand and was still buried in a tomb hundreds of miles away when the Irish text was written. However, Old Irish and Gaulish are related languages and they share some inherited vocabulary. It is not unreasonable that they might also have shared magical phraseology, either from a common ancestral stage in the history of the Celtic languages or (perhaps more likely) because the inherited words for 'magic' and 'women' alliterate, and alliteration makes for good poetry.

Ritual aimed at warding off evil powers is known as 'apotropaic', a word that comes from Greek and literally means 'turning away from' – the idea being that someone could use a ritual object or process to deflect or ward off any evil that might be coming their way. The *lorica* ascribed to St Patrick is not the only medieval one to be connected with a particular Irish saint. There are *loricae* associated with the Irish saint Fursa as well as the 6th-century CE authors Laidcenn and Gildas. The *loricae* of saints Patrick and Fursa are written in Irish and could have been accessible to a wider range of people beyond the monks and the monastery. By contrast, the *lorica* of Laidcenn (sometimes also attributed to Gildas, the British monk and writer) was composed in Latin, which would have limited its readership to those living or at least trained in a monastic context (more on this *lorica* in the next chapter). Of course, everyday people could have still recited or memorized a Latin text even if they did not know Latin well (or at all) themselves. If we recall from Chapter 2 that magical words were often found on amulets or curse tablets in the ancient world, we are reminded that someone scarcely needed to understand a text to use it for magical purposes.

Loricae associated with saints were not the only religious texts that held miraculous powers. In several medieval Irish texts, the act of repeating Psalm 119 (called the *Beati* after its opening word in the Latin Bible) is shown to rescue someone's soul from hell. Such

Christ is depicted enthroned on this richly illuminated page from the Book of Kells, *c.* 800 CE.

St Patrick's *lorica*

If you fear evil forces are looming, you can try reciting this excerpt from the *lorica* of St Patrick to keep them at bay.

I bind to myself today,
The Power of God to guide me,
The Might of God to uphold me,
The Wisdom of God to teach me,
The Eye of God to watch over me,
The Ear of God to hear me,
The Word of God to give me speech,
The Hand of God to protect me,
The Way of God to prevent me,
The Shield of God to shelter me,
The Host of God to defend me,
Against the snares of demons,
Against the temptations of vices,
Against the lusts of nature,
Against every man who meditates injury to me,
Whether far or near,
With few or with many.
I have set around me all these powers,
Against every hostile savage power,
Directed against my body and my soul,
Against the incantations of false prophets,
Against the black laws of heathenism,
Against the false laws of heresy,
Against the deceits of idolatry,
Against the spells of women and smiths and druids,
Against all knowledge which harms the soul of man.

episodes offer benign counterparts to the sorts of maledictory uses of the Psalms seen above, recited by angry saints to punish evildoers or to get their own way. In one story, a young cleric gets a nun pregnant in contravention of their vows of celibacy. The nun dies in childbirth and the cleric vows to save her soul. He eventually accomplishes this by reciting the *Beati* seven times a day for several years. Another medieval Irish poem states that whoever recites the sweet *Beati* every day and night will receive glory and grace and banish vice. The poem even refers to the *Beati* as 'a *lorica* for soul and body' and a 'shield against every evil'.

Many *lorica*-like charms that were used for medical purposes also survive from medieval Ireland and Britain and we will encounter some of these in the next chapter. Just like the miracles and magic discussed here, we will see that the boundaries between prayer, magic and medicine were also blurred for most medieval authors and audiences. For most medieval people, these were all parts of nature and existed within the parameters of God's creation. God's power allowed the faithful to understand and shape the world around them, whether through praying to saints like Patrick, Columba, Brigit, Cadog, or David, or preparing a herbal remedy to drive a headache away.

5

MEDICAL MAGIC AND ASTROLOGY

Wales, 14th century.

For a snakebite: Take a live chicken (preferably a cock) and pluck the feathers from its anus. Hold its anus to the wound. Hold it there until the chicken has died. Repeat as necessary until all the poison has been drawn out.

Bizarre as it may sound, the procedure summarized above was a relatively common medieval European treatment for snakebites and even plague buboes. Applying the anus of the chicken directly to the location of the bite was supposed to draw the poison out of the wound (and into the bird). Presumably after the chicken (or chickens) had absorbed all the poison, and died in the process, the patient would be cured. This treatment appears in several collections of medical recipes written in medieval Welsh found in manuscripts dating from the 14th and 15th centuries. This collection of Welsh medical material was traditionally attributed to the *Meddygon Myddfai*, the semi-legendary Physicians of Myddfai, located in Carmarthenshire, south-west Wales. The Physicians of Myddfai were supposedly a family of medical practitioners descended from Rhiwallon the Physician, who ministered to Rhys Gryg, prince of the kingdom of Deheubarth in southern Wales, in the 13th century. Folklore claims that Rhiwallon had three sons, named Cadwgan, Gruffudd and Einion, who carried on his medical teachings and that the family survived into the 17th century. The Physicians of Myddfai attained legendary status but many more mundane families of professional physicians worked in both Ireland and Wales, and transmitted their knowledge across

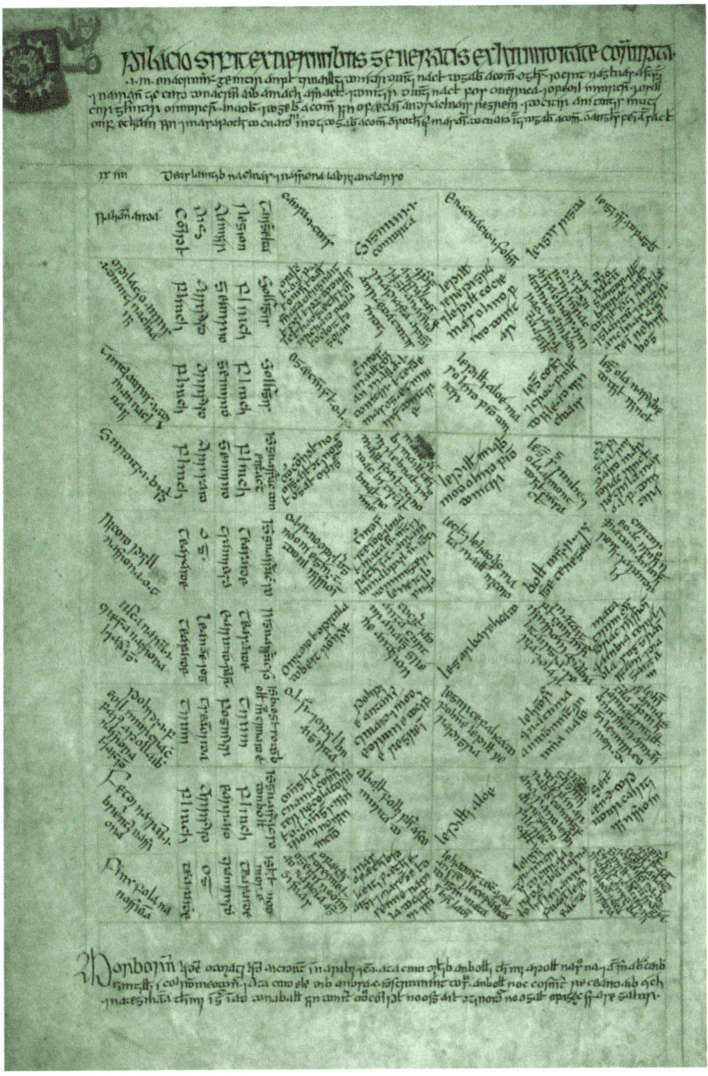

A medical table from the 15th-century *Book of O'Lees*, which details the names, symptoms, prognoses and cures of various diseases.

generations. Collections of medical recipes and procedures compiled and owned by these families often bear their names, such as *Book of O'Lees* and the *Liber Flavus Fergusiorum* ('The Yellow Book of the Ferguses'), which belonged respectively to two medical families working in Connacht in the west of Ireland in the later Middle Ages.

Modern scholars now recognize that most of the recipes found in medieval Welsh medical compendia in fact represent an international approach to medical care that spanned the medieval world from Persian- and Arabic-speaking areas through northwestern Europe. This medical tradition drew upon classical Greco-Roman authors

This 17th-century oil painting is thought to depict the Muslim physician Ibn Sīnā (*c.* 980–1037), one of the most influential medical writers of the Middle Ages.

Chicken soup is a popular remedy for colds today, but medieval medical uses of chickens can be surprising!

such as Galen and Hippocrates as well as the 10th- and 11th-century Muslim physician Ibn Sīnā (Avicenna). Medieval medical texts were transmitted and re-transmitted throughout the Mediterranean, the Near East, North Africa and Europe. Medical treatises survive in almost every language written during the Middle Ages.

Today most people make a distinction between 'medicine' and 'magic' but this was not always the case. The example of the snakebite treatment above, surreal as it seems, details a straightforward enough process that involves a medical procedure (affixing the correct part of the chicken onto the snakebite) and at least one ingredient (the chicken). However, plenty of medical recipes also included an oral component, in addition to medicinal ingredients and physical procedures. These oral elements were somewhere between everyday prayers, the protective *loricae* seen in the previous chapter and ritual charms.

For example, a cure for fever from a medieval Welsh medical manuscript stipulates:

> Drink rue juice mixed with wine, swallow coriander seeds and drink wild celery mixed with water.... Collect greater

> plantain while saying your Paternoster and drink that mixed with wine as well.

In this case, is the cure brought about by the consumption of the herbal remedy, the recitation of the Paternoster (the Latin prayer beginning 'Our Father...'), or some combination of the two? Clearly medieval authors and readers thought recipes like this were effective, whatever the source of their power. Usually, a doctor's procedure, a spoken charm or prayer, and divine goodwill were not seen as opposing forces; instead, a combination of these elements might contribute to a patient's healing. This is not unlike a modern person today who mumbles a pseudo-medical dictum such as 'An apple a day keeps the doctor away' and prays for the good health of a friend or relative, all while turning up for a yearly check-up with their physician.

Do these cures for snakebite and fever constitute magic? Take our original definition of magic as 'The use of ritual activities or observances which are intended to influence the course of events or to manipulate the natural world, usually involving the use of an occult or secret body of knowledge'. Medieval medical recipes like these certainly qualify as types of 'ritual activities intended to influence the course of events'. In this case, the ritual activities included gathering the proper ingredients in the first place and following the steps of the recipe. Influencing the course of events in a medical context meant bringing about the patient's recovery.

Was this knowledge 'secret or occult'? Access to the information in these recipes was restricted to those with access to the correct manuscripts, the ability to read one or more languages and, perhaps more importantly, the professional knowledge required to turn a list of ingredients and a vague description of a process into a viable medical procedure. In this respect, medieval medical knowledge was at least highly specialized and sometimes obscure, if not outright

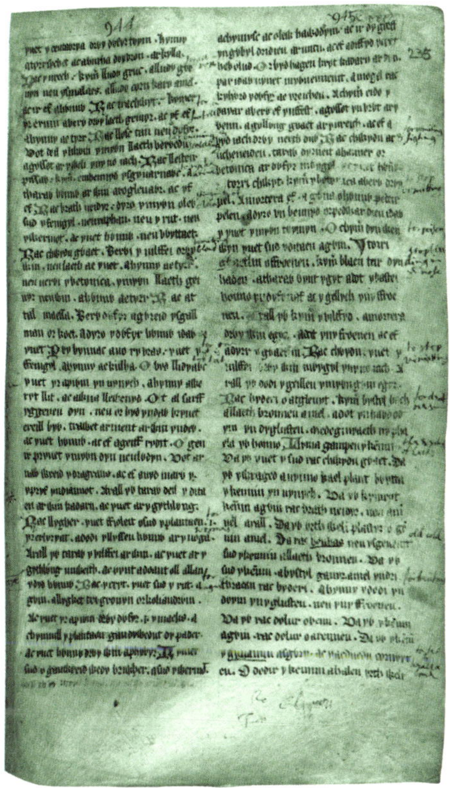

A medieval Welsh medical tract from the *Red Book of Hergest*, now in Jesus College, Oxford.

secret. There is also much that is not included in the recipes that a practitioner would have to already know in order to follow their directions. This information may not have been secret per se, but it could only be gained through practical experience or by watching other physicians at work, so it was exclusive knowledge. For example, medieval medical recipes rarely contain specific quantities or ratios of ingredients and this would have had to be worked out by the

A charm against headache

This Latin charm was probably written by a medieval Irish author. Like some of the other *lorica* and medical charms we have seen, it invokes various Biblical characters, linking each to a part of the body. Next time you have a headache, drink a glass of water, take some painkillers and give it a try.

Against a headache, sing the following every day:
Christ's head
Isaiah's eye
Elijah's forehead
Noah's nose
Job's lips
Solomon's tongue
Matthew's neck
Benjamin's thought
Paul's chest
John's grace
Abraham's faith
Abel's blood
Holy, Holy, Holy,
God Lord of Hosts. Amen.

Spit twice into your hand and put the saliva on your temples and on the back of your head. Sing the Paternoster three times. Draw a cross made of your saliva on the top of your head and make a U shape on your head.

physician. Similarly, medical texts often prescribe certain procedures such as a cautery (applying heat to a wound in a controlled fashion in order to sear and sterilize damaged tissue) without providing step-by-step instructions. Anyone working from these texts probably already had a fundamental knowledge of how to carry out certain procedures or brew remedies.

Some protective prayers are also almost medical in their terminology. For instance, the *lorica* of Laidcenn (which is sometimes

– almost certainly incorrectly – ascribed to the authorship of the 6th-century British saint Gildas) contains the following anatomical descriptions:

Lord be you safest lorica,
for my limbs, for my entrails,
that you may thrust back from me the invisible
nails of stakes, which enemies fashion.
Cover, therefore, O God, with strong corslet,
along with shoulder blades, shoulders and arms.
Cover elbows with elbow-joints and hands,
fists, palms, fingers with their nails.
Cover back-bone and ribs with their joints,
hind-parts, back, nerves and bones.
Cover surface, blood and kidneys,
haunches, buttocks with the thighs.
Cover hams, calves, thighs,
kneecaps, hamstrings and knees.
Cover ankles, shins and heels,
legs, feet with the rests of the soles....

The whole *lorica* is much longer and invokes divine aid, like the *loricae* seen in the last chapter, but this excerpt gives a sense of the overlap between protective prayer and medical learning. By naming the varied body parts in the *lorica*, the speaker sought God's aid in averting illness or injury to these areas and to their body as a whole.

This charm was reasonably popular, as versions of it survive in multiple medieval manuscripts from Ireland, England and Switzerland. (Irish missionaries and monks were active across continental Europe in the early Middle Ages, so it is not surprising to find the occasional Irish text turning up outside Ireland.)

UNIVERSAL MEDICINE

In many respects, medieval medicine practised in Celtic-speaking areas by the central and later Middle Ages looked very similar to medieval medicine practised elsewhere in Europe, the Mediterranean, the Near East and North Africa. Very little about it was any more distinctively 'Celtic' than it was 'Latin' or 'Arabic' or 'Greek' or 'Persian'. Most of these similarities were due to shared collections of medical information that circulated in translation. Physicians could also travel to centres of medical expertise such as Salerno in southern Italy to learn their craft. Medical knowledge spread through the movement of both people and books. Jewish, Muslim and Christian scholars were all important contributors to the translation and dissemination of medical knowledge during the Middle Ages. As recently as 2019, a new fragment of a 15th-century Irish-language translation of Ibn Sīnā's *Canon of Medicine* made the news when it was rediscovered tucked into the binding of a later book at University College Cork.

The core philosophy behind most medieval medicine was 'humoral': the idea that the human body contained four types of fluids or humours that needed to be kept in careful balance. These humours were blood, red or yellow bile, black bile and phlegm. Some humours were considered to be hot (blood, red/yellow bile), while others were cold (black bile, phlegm), some were dry (red/yellow bile, black bile), while others were moist (blood, phlegm). In addition to four humours, medieval medicine recognized four temperaments linked to the humours that described different human personalities: sanguine (characterized by an excess of blood), choleric (an excess of red/yellow bile), melancholic (an excess of black bile) and phlegmatic (an excess of phlegm). Someone who was deemed to have an excessively sanguine temperament might have their blood let to adjust their humoral balance or they might be proscribed medicine or food that had the opposite qualities to blood: blood was hot and moist,

A 15th-century fragment of an Irish translation of Ibn Sīnā's *Canon of Medicine*, reused as part of the binding of another book.

so ingredients or procedures that promoted cold, dry qualities could counter its effects. Both humoral theory and the four temperaments had their roots in ancient Greek and Roman medical philosophy and were later refined by scientists in the Islamic world.

Despite this common framework for medieval medical thought, regional differences still existed. Translators tripped over unfamiliar words for flora and fauna in their source texts and sometimes local plants or ingredients had to be substituted for foreign equivalents that did not grow locally. Particularly popular medicinal plants in medieval Wales included yarrow (*Achillea millefolium*) and mugwort (*Artemisia vulgaris*) but a few recipes even call for saffron (*Crocus*

The four humoural temperaments (clockwise from top left): Sanguine, Choleric, Phlegmatic and Melancholic, from an engraving, *c.* 1590.

sativus), which is highly labour intensive to grow and harvest. One recommends: 'If you want to be happy always, eat saffron in food or drink and you will never be sad. But beware of eating too much in case you die of happiness'. (Of course, anyone who could regularly afford to consume expensive spices like saffron might have already had a head start when it came to happiness.) A warning against achieving too much happiness might sound ridiculous to modern ears, but we must remember that the goal of medieval humoral theory was to maintain balance. Too much of anything (happiness or otherwise) could cause imbalance in the body and cause poor health and disease.

In addition to shared recipe collections and knowledge spread by travelling texts and physicians, some charm formulas also look very similar across different medieval traditions. It has been observed that many languages in the Indo-European language family share certain medical charm phrasing. In a 9th-century Irish text, we find a doctor setting 'joint against joint...and sinew against sinew'. This sounds very similar to an Old High German charm, also from about the 9th century, in which the god Woden cures a horse by putting 'bone to bone, blood to blood, limb to limb'. In the *Atharvaveda*, a religious text from India from the 2nd millennium BCE, we also encounter a god putting together 'marrow with marrow, skin with skin, blood with blood, flesh with flesh' and more. Versions of similar charms can be found as far removed as Scotland and the Baltic.

Medieval herbal remedies called for ingredients such as saffron (left) and mugwort (right).

A hypothetical medieval Irish person who travelled to the monastery of Fulda in Germany, where the Old High German charm was probably written down in the 10th century, could have recognized it as akin to their own medical traditions. Scholars have suggested that these types of charms represent a very old formula present in Proto-Indo-European many thousands of years ago and shared among many descendant Indo-European languages. It is also possible that some of these similarities are merely the result of chance or reflect regional traditions that spread between neighbouring languages at a later date. Whatever the origins of these charms, they reflect shared medical and magical impulses to put like together with like in order to heal the whole. The appeal to a higher power to put 'like with like' might have been accompanied by the real setting of broken bones or stitching together of flesh, or it might have been intended to ward off such injuries in the first place.

Hangover cures

Several medieval Welsh medical collections suggest antidotes for over-indulging in alcohol...

How to avoid getting drunk:

Drink an eggshell of the juice of betony in the morning.

How to sober up quickly:

Eat saffron crushed with spring water.

How to get rid of a headache if you failed to follow the advice above:

Pound garlic, onion and goat fat in a mortar and bandage it around the head. Leave it for eight days. Then boil oats in water for a long time. Wash the bandage off the head with the warm oat and water mixture. Repeat until the headache is healed.

You should check with your doctor before you try any such herbal remedies yourself (especially if you are already taking any medications).

OLD IRISH IN OLD ENGLISH CHARMS AND OLD ENGLISH IN OLD IRISH CHARMS

Charms spread between Ireland and Britain during the medieval period as well. A well-known Old English medical collection called the *Lacnunga* (Old English for 'Remedies') found in a late 10th-century manuscript contains several charms written partly in Old Irish. One of these charms offers a remedy against worms. The medical practitioner is to sing the following charm nine times in the afflicted person's ear, followed by the Paternoster: '*gonomil orgomil marbumil*'. These words are slightly garbled Old Irish for 'I wound the beast,

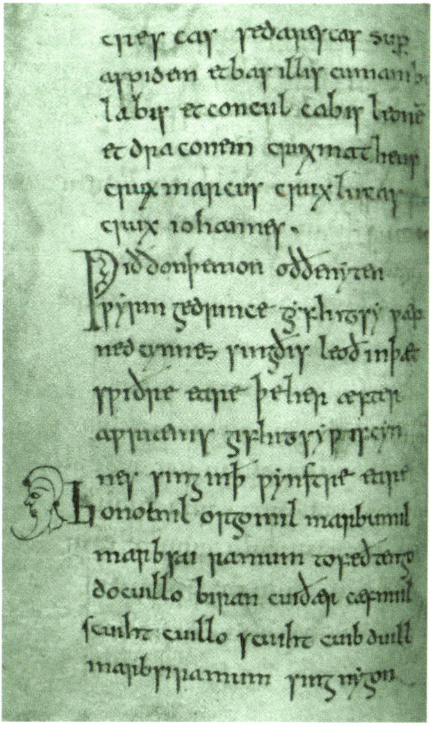

The beginning of a garbled Old Irish charm is marked by the face in the margins of the *Lacnunga*.

I strike the beast, I kill the beast'. Like the charms we saw earlier, its efficacy is amplified by the inclusion of the Paternoster prayer. This produces a trilingual incantation including instructions and phrases in Old English, Old Irish and Latin.

It is common to find the occasional Greek or Hebrew word or phrase in medieval charms, although in early medieval Ireland and Britain very few people knew more than a few words of Greek or Hebrew. The use of multiple languages or nonsense words gave an

This manuscript of an Old English herbal contains lists of useful herbs and remedies along with illustrations of some of the plants and animals included in recipes.

A charm against urinary disease

This Irish-language charm against urinary infection appears in the same manuscript from Switzerland as the Irish headache charm. Like some of the examples above, it includes a line of garbled Latin and Greek words to add extra mystical power. In this case, the Latin and Greek comes from the Bible (Matthew 28:18): 'Go therefore, and teach all nations, baptizing them in the name of the Father, and of the Son, and of the Holy Ghost'. In addition to providing suitably mystical-sounding words, this line also invokes the salvific power of the Gospels.

I save myself from this disease of urine,
a cattle-goad saves us,
skillful bird-flocks of spell-workers save us.
This is always put where you urinate.
Presinitphsan omnybus knaatyonibus
End.

If you are sufferring from a urinary infection it's worth a try, although we would also recommend consulting a 21st-century pharmacist or physician.

incantation power, much like the ancient curses that are sometimes multilingual or use magical gibberish. By expressing a sentiment or request in multiple languages or in gibberish, practitioners could express the ineffable and harness the power of the unseen. If the languages in question had religious or occult significance, so much the better. Thus, in the Middle Ages, the languages of scripture (for medieval Christians, Latin, Greek and Hebrew) held special power because of their link to the divine.

Most Old Irish words in the Old English medical charms are mangled badly in the versions that survive today. Presumably at some point the authors of the Old English charms had a general idea of what the Old Irish bits meant (or at least knew that they were effective against certain ailments). However, by the time these Irish words were copied down in the English manuscripts in which they survive today, they might have been interpreted as mystical nonsense words rather than understood in their original Irish meaning. These multilingual charms provide evidence that medical knowledge and magical charms crossed the Irish Sea at an early date.

Charms also travelled across the Irish Sea in the other direction. Several Old English words are preserved in Irish medical charms, including one multilingual bloodletting charm that reads '*egor egor memor memor tap tap cep cep*'. For an Irish-speaking audience, these unfamiliar Old English words probably served the same mystical purpose as the Irish words in the Old English charm did for an Old English-speaking audience. However, they also seem to have some bearing on the topic at hand: in Old English, *egor* refers to something like 'stream' or 'flood' (presumably a stream of blood in the context of the charm); *tap* instructs the reader to draw a liquid (in this context, blood); *memor* is a Latin word meaning 'mindful'; and *cep* is another Old English instruction to the reader to be observant. So the whole line tells the reader to be observant and mindful about letting the patient's blood. Even if a later reader did not know what the Old English words themselves meant, the words imbued the charm with mystical authority.

ASTROLOGY AND MEDICINE

In addition to a person's primary humours and temperament, the ruling planet under which they were born and their zodiac sign provided information that was considered important for understanding their character and treating them if they fell ill. A modern-day reader may be surprised to learn that these medieval zodiac signs are more or less the same as they are in many places today and include familiar signs like Capricorn and Sagittarius. Medieval astrology, like medical recipes, was widespread and both Celtic speakers and non-Celtic

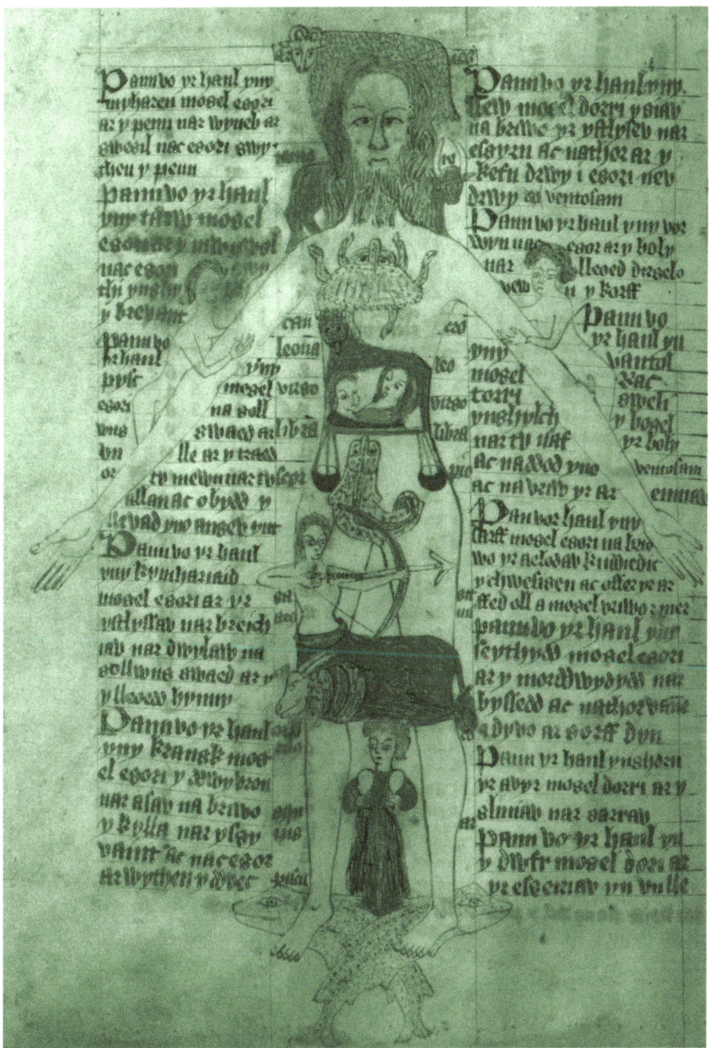

A Zodiac Man diagram from a medieval Welsh manuscript, 1488–89. The twelve astrological symbols are shown alongside the body part they correspond to. For example, the fish of Pisces are shown next to the feet.

speakers across Europe and beyond would have shared sets of zodiac signs based on Greco-Roman names for the constellations and similar ideas about how they influenced personality and physical health. While these astrological practices are not distinctively 'Celtic', we do have astrological texts surviving in medieval Celtic languages.

Many medieval and early modern manuscripts include diagrams of the *Homo Signorum* ('Man of Signs') or 'Zodiac Man', which was ultimately based on medical and astrological learning from the ancient Mediterranean world. These diagrams depict a human body covered with zodiac signs. Each sign corresponds to a particular body part or region, although the exact correspondences could vary between diagrams. From looking at one of these diagrams, a physician could tell the optimal time to treat certain diseases or perform particular procedures. For instance, on these diagrams the feet are often associated with the sign of Pisces. Thus, the part of the year governed by Pisces (between mid-February and mid-March, when the sun appears in this constellation) might have been an opportune time for foot surgery.

A well-known Zodiac Man in a medieval Welsh manuscript dating from the 15th century links the zodiac signs to the following body parts:

Aries: head
Taurus: neck
Gemini: shoulders
Cancer: chest
Leo: stomach
Virgo: abdomen
Libra: hips, buttocks
Scorpio: genitals
Sagittarius: thighs
Capricorn: knees
Aquarius: calves
Pisces: feet

This was a common scheme reflected across medieval Zodiac diagrams. On the Welsh diagram, Scorpio looks a little like a snake – perhaps not surprising given that 1) the Welsh word used for the constellation Scorpio (*sarff*) usually means 'snake', and 2) most people in medieval Wales had probably never seen a scorpion.

If you lived in medieval Wales, you could also consult specific texts to find out what was in store for your star sign, just like you can read the horoscope column in the newspaper or visit an astrology website nowadays. Indeed, some of these medieval texts list other

Medieval astrological signs (clockwise from top left):
Leo, Virgo, Scorpio and Libra.

signs that you are likely to be compatible with and others signs that you should avoid. Horoscopes were sometimes split by gender: a girl born under a certain sign might have a different future than a boy born under the same sign. For instance, one medieval Welsh astrological text called the *Llyfr y Dynghedfen* ('Book of Destiny') or *Llyfr Naturiaeth* ('Book of Disposition') claims that male Capricorns

---

A medieval Welsh horoscope

Here are some late medieval Welsh astrological predictions. How do they compare with horoscopes today?

Leo (the Lion)

And the boy who is born under the sign which is called the Lion (that is, from mid-July to mid-August) will be skilful and gracious and amiable... he will be very merciful and compassionate to his neighbours...and he will get a wound from the tooth of a dog but it will not hurt him and, because of his nature, his life-span will be eighty-four years....

And the girl born under this sign will be fair and broad and very strong but merciful and her speech will be feminine...and she will have children from three men...and she will get a wound from the tooth of a dog and she will get a fall from a high place and from thirty-six years on she will start [to get] good things and happiness....

Virgo (the Maiden)

And the boy who is born under the sign called the Maiden (that is, from the middle of August until the middle of September) will be mild and calm and feminine and he will not be greatly feared but he will be bitter and stubborn and his speech will be fair....

And the girl born under this sign will be weary and hard-working in the world and will not be amiable with a man...and she should live until she may be sixty years old and, because of her nature, she should take a ring with a miraculous stone in it and the stone will be miraculous and keep her from danger....

---

are said to be sharp and talkative (perhaps gossips?) by nature while Capricorn women are easy-going and well-liked.

The same text goes into minute levels of detail in places and even includes several predictions about signs who will be bitten by dogs ('A Medieval Welsh Horoscope' provides an example). This was evidently a regular occurrence in 15th-century Wales and while

---

Libra (the Weights)

And the boy who is born under the sign which is called the Weights (that is, from mid-September until mid-October) will be capable and honourable in his childhood and he will travel to many different places among foreigners and he will be accepted among the best [people]....

And the girl who is born under this sign will be pure and loving and amiable and she will get happiness over her adversaries and she will travel with strangers in other lands and she will be amiable and generous and famous....

Scorpio (the Scorpion)

And the boy who is born under the sign which is called the Scorpion [or, Snake] (that is from mid-October to mid-November) will get many good chances and will be a great planner upon the world ... he will love merriment and musicians but because of his nature he should get illness from pain ....

And the girl born under this sign will be feminine and amiable and full of vanity and her first husband – there will not be much agreement between them but she will still get happiness from him and great kindness and long-lasting harmony ....

---

many of us may worry less about dog bites today, injury caused by canines was clearly a medieval concern, as demonstrated by this 8th-century Irish medical charm:

I smite sickness,
I smite wounding,
I halt swelling,
I heal sickness.
Against the hound which seizes.
Against the thorn which pierces.
Against the iron which strikes.

Medieval horoscopes, just like their modern counterparts, are often somewhat vague, allowing readers to read whatever they want into their predictions. In the course of a person's life, they would probably have encountered at least one aggressive dog (although this probably had less to do with someone's star sign than with everyday reality).

PREDICTING LIFE AND DEATH

One of magic's great uses is 'prognostication' (predicting the future). This is obviously important in a medical context. Horoscopes sometimes predicted a person's lifespan but there were other rituals you could use if you wanted more immediate information about someone's chances of survival and recovery. If you wanted to know if a sick person was going to die in medieval Wales, you had several ways to find out. One method involved pounding violets and applying the resulting mash to the ailing person's temples. If the patient fell asleep, they would live, but if they could not sleep, they would die. A variant on this procedure involved putting the horn of a goat underneath the afflicted's head. If they subsequently slept, they would recover; if they did not, they would die. Alternatively, one could write the names of the Seven Sleepers on the hilt of a knife, and, again, place it under the ill person's head without their knowledge. Whether they would live or die could be determined based on their ability to sleep.

The Seven Sleepers were a group of legendary early Christians who hid in a cave to avoid persecution in the 3rd century CE. In most versions of the story, the cave was said to be located near Ephesus, an ancient city close to modern-day Selçuk, Türkiye. The mouth of the cave was sealed and the sleepers fell into a miraculous sleep. Several centuries later the mouth of the cave was opened and the sleepers awoke, thinking they had slept for a single day. They emerged from the cave and were surprised to find that the coins they tried to spend in the marketplace were hundreds of years old. They finally died and went to heaven, having escaped martyrdom in order to share their miraculous story with people in later ages. In a few versions of the story, the sleepers also have a pet dog. The story of the Seven Sleepers was very popular in the Middle Ages with both Christian and Muslim audiences. Given the manipulation of time in the story and the miraculous slumber that saves the Seven Sleepers from martyrdom, it is perhaps not surprising to find it included in a medical prognostication ritual aimed at determining how long a patient would live. The names of the sleepers vary a bit between sources, but if you want to try the Welsh ritual and you have a suitable knife, you can use this relatively common version of their names: Maximianus, Malchus, Johannes, Martinianus, Constantinus, Dionysius and Serapion.

Life and death in the past were unpredictable, just as they are today. People tried to influence health and illness as best they could, through remedies, prayer and astrological knowledge. When a friend or family member was sick, they worried and wondered about their recovery, and so they turned to magical methods to determine whether

A 19th-century icon painting of the Seven Sleepers of Ephesus.
Pet dog not pictured.

a patient was likely to recover or not. Such techniques were obviously not foolproof, but they offered a modicum of certainty in an unpredictable universe. Like many people still do, people in the Middle Ages turned to their faith to get them through difficult times, heal injuries and diseases and ultimately save their souls after death. Most medieval speakers of Celtic languages were Christians who anticipated resurrection on Judgement Day: concern for one's health in this world was matched by concern for one's soul in the next.

6

MAGICIANS IN MEDIEVAL LITERATURE

Newgrange, Ireland. The legendary past.

Once upon a time, a long time ago the Dagda ruled over Ireland. One of his duties was to divide up the síd mounds of Ireland between the various members of his family, the Túatha Dé, so that they would each have somewhere to live. The síde were wonderful places. In the Dagda's own home, the Brug (Newgrange), trees bore fruit all year long and spits of roasting meat and barrels of drink were never empty.

However, the Dagda had forgotten to set a síd aside for one of the Túatha Dé: the Mac Óc. One day the Mac Óc came to see the Dagda, asking for a dwelling of his own. The síde had all been allocated by this point, however, and the Dagda turned him away. Disappointed, the Mac Óc begged the Dagda for permission to spend a day and a night in the Brug. The Dagda agreed to this harmless request. When the Dagda turned up the next morning to turn the Mac Óc out of his house, however, he realized he had been tricked: the Mac Óc pointed out, he had been given day and night in the Brug and since all time passes in increments of day and night, by rights the Brug was his forever. The Dagda could not argue with this logic and left the Brug to the Mac Óc, where he remains to this day, feasting on eternal fruit and roast pork.

OTHERWORLDLY PEOPLE AND PLACES

In medieval Irish literature, a *síd* (plural *síde*) is a mound that opens onto a fantastic Otherworld full of marvellous items and supernatural beings. Sometimes *síd* is translated as 'fairy mound' and *síde* still play an important role in Irish fairytales and folklore today. The story of the Dagda and the Mac Óc is based on a tale called *The Taking of the Síd* from roughly the 8th century, which tells how the *síde* were distributed among a family of supernatural characters in the distant past. In the story, the Mac Óc (literally, 'young son', also called Óengus in Irish literature) tricks the Dagda out of his home by asking to stay for 'day and night'. The Dagda interprets this as a single day and night, but medieval Irish lacks an indefinite article (the equivalent of 'a' or 'some' in English), so it is ambiguous whether the Mac Óc means a single day and night or day and night generally. When the Dagda tries to send him on his way the next morning, the Mac Óc argues that he meant the latter and, because all time passes

Construction of Newgrange predated the arrival of Celtic speakers in Ireland by millennia but medieval authors were deeply curious about its origins.

in increments of days and nights, the *síd* is his for evermore. The *síd* in question is called the Brug or Brú na Boinne, the Irish name for the prehistoric monument in County Meath, Ireland, known today as Newgrange.

The Mac Óc's clever play on words is perhaps its own type of magic that works on other magic-workers themselves. In other versions of the story, the magical element is more explicit: the Dagda sleeps with Boand, who is married to another man, and the Mac Óc is the product of their adultery. In order to hide the pregnancy from Boand's husband, the Dagda halts the progress of the sun in the sky for nine months so that it seems like no time at all has passed. The Mac Óc engages in similar temporal trickery when he obtains the *síd* for himself through ambiguous wordplay later in the tale.

Medieval literature in Celtic languages is replete with Otherworldly locations and characters and clever wordplay that verges upon magic. In the first of four medieval Welsh tales called the *Four Branches of the Mabinogi*, the prince Pwyll encounters a character named Arawn,

Pwyll and his servants chase after Rhiannon, illustration from John Young Evans's *The Pwyll Pendefig Dyfed*, 1922.

who is the king of an Otherworldly land called Annwn. Pwyll swaps kingdoms with Arawn for a year and earns Arawn's respect and friendship after ruling Annwn well and refusing to sleep with Arawn's wife during this time. Later, Pwyll encounters another Otherworldly woman named Rhiannon whom he races on horseback. Pwyll too becomes the victim of ambiguous wordplay and loses Rhiannon to another suitor when he foolishly promises the other man anything he wants. Pwyll eventually gets her back, loses her again and regains her a final time. It is probably no accident that *pwyll* means 'wisdom' or 'prudence' in Welsh – over the course of the tale, the titular character gradually learns how to be wise.

Depictions of Otherworlds and Otherworldly inhabitants in medieval Celtic literature are many and varied. They span Irish paradisiacal *síde* where trees always bear fruit, Arawn's Annwn (which seems to be a distant yet accessible version of our own world) and even mysterious places like Avalon, where some authors claimed the legendary King Arthur was taken after being wounded in his final battle. There is no single 'Celtic' Otherworld, just as there is no single Celtic culture, literary tradition or medieval language. Instead, we are treated to a panoply of paradises, each one of which is unique and operates by its own set of rules.

The powerful and sometimes immortal inhabitants of the Otherworld in medieval Irish literature are often known as the Aes Síde ('People of the *Síd*'), the Túatha Dé Danann ('Peoples of the Goddess Danu') or the Túatha Dé ('God Peoples'). At various points in Irish literature, the Túatha Dé fight against other families of supernatural beings, including the Fomorians and the Fir Bolg. Members of all three groups are sometimes interpreted as medieval survivors from the pre-Christian gods of Ireland and some of the characters themselves do have names that include words for 'god' (such as the Dagda, whose name literally means the 'good god'). The names of other characters are related to those of continental Celtic gods like those we saw earlier (for example, the names of Lug in Irish tales and Lleu in Welsh literature parallel the Gaulish god Lugus). As discussed briefly in the first chapter, however, no written-down myths survive from pre-Christian Ireland or Britain and so we do not know whether or not these medieval characters actually reflect pre-Christian Irish or British deities. Medieval texts very rarely treat supernatural characters as gods. Instead, medieval literature furnishes them with genealogies that go back to Biblical characters, such as Noah, and portray them as subject to the will of the Christian God. In some stories they appear as supernatural heroes and helpers, while in other texts they are said to be demons. There were probably as many different interpretations of the Otherworld and its inhabitants as there were medieval authors and readers.

Whatever else the tales discussed here may or may not be, they were all the deliberate and intentional work of creative authors. Just

In John Duncan's romanticized paining, 1911, the inhabitants of the *síd* hover somewhere between medieval fables and the pre-Christian past.

as someone today may pick up a book about dragons in the library, watch a supernatural horror film in the cinema or sit down to play a fantasy role-playing game with their friends, medieval readers were capable of enjoying fantastic settings without necessarily believing that they reflected reality. Much like people now, people in the Middle Ages enjoyed a good story! Some Celtic speakers of the past were probably more willing to believe in fantastical stories or seek magical solutions than others. Someone might trust in their horoscope but laugh at implausible stories about shapeshifting magicians. Someone else might accept that their ancestors had defeated a supernatural

Macha curses the Ulstermen, illustration from Eleanor Hull's *The Boys' Cuchulain: Heroic Legends of Ireland*, 1904.

A banishing charm

Do you want to get rid of unwelcome neighbours? Or convince someone to vacate a house that you think really ought to belong to you? Try this banishing charm, which appears in several medieval Irish texts. In one narrative called *Cath Maige Tuired* ('The Second Battle of Moytura') from about the 9th century the spell rouses the Túatha Dé to fight in a battle in which they expel the rival Fomorians from their lands. In another late medieval version of the story about the Mac Óc and Newgrange, it is used to help the Mac Óc acquire the *síd* through trickery.

Proclaim that your enemies cannot return:

...until Ogma and his hound come together, until heaven and earth come together, until sun and moon come together.

The charm, if successful, should ensure a banishment that lasts a good long time!

(Ogma, invoked here, is a member of the Túatha Dé and in some medieval texts he is associated with the creation of the ogam alphabet – more on this later. Ogma has been connected to the Gaulish god Ogmios but the degree to which the medieval Irish character and the Gaulish deity are related is uncertain.)

race of Otherworldly sorcerers but doubt that attaching a live chicken to a snakebite would cure the injury. Trusting in one kind of magic or practising a particular ritual did not guarantee that someone would treat another type of magic or ritual in the same way.

As we saw from Pwyll's decidedly mixed Otherworldly bag, interactions with the Otherworld did not always go well for mortals. The medieval Welsh poem *Preiddeu Annwn* ('The Spoils of Annwn') narrates a disastrous trip led by King Arthur to an Otherworldly fortress across the sea, from which only seven adventurers return. In *Immram Brain* ('The Voyage of Bran'), an Irish story from about the 8th century, Bran and his crew go on a marvellous Otherworldly voyage to a sinless land inhabited by women. After some time, one of the crew becomes homesick and they return to Ireland, only to find that centuries have passed at home during their absence in the Otherworld. One of Bran's crew jumps ashore and is reduced to a heap of dust. Bran and the rest of the crew narrate their adventures (wisely from the safety of their boat) before sailing off again to parts unknown.

In another medieval Irish tale called *Noínden Ulad* ('The Debility of the Ulstermen'), an Otherworldly woman named Macha marries a mortal man and lives quietly with him. One day, her husband foolishly brags about her supernatural swiftness to the king of Ulster, who forces Macha to race against his best horses in order to prove that her husband's wild claims are true. Macha asks for the contest to be delayed because she is heavily pregnant at the time but the king threatens to kill her husband on the spot unless she complies. Macha runs the race and wins but collapses and gives birth on the finish line. Humiliated, Macha curses the Ulstermen for nine generations to feel the pains of childbirth at the least convenient moment. She declares:

> From this time onwards the dishonour you have inflicted upon me will be a disgrace for you. When it may be most difficult for you, you will only have the strength of a woman in labour for anyone who guards the province [of Ulster]; and the period of time that a woman is in labour is the period of time that you will be [afflicted], that is until the end of five days and four nights, and it will be upon you also for nine generations, that is for the [life]time of nine men.

Macha's curse strikes years later when Queen Medb and King Ailill of Connacht come to raid Ulster, as narrated in the medieval Irish epic *Táin Bó Cúailnge* ('The Cattle Raid of Cooley'). The adult men defending Ulster are gripped by labour pains and cannot fight. After generations, Macha gets the last laugh.

John Duncan strikes again with an even more romanticized impression of the medieval literary character Óengus (the Mac Óc), 1908.

THE POWER OF DREAMS

As we saw earlier in the healing shrines of the classical world, where the dreams of sick people were interpreted in order to find out what was wrong, dreams provided one way in which characters in medieval literature interacted with Otherworldly figures and powers. In a medieval Welsh text called *Breuddwyd Macsen* ('The Dream of Macsen'), the Roman emperor Magnus Maximus (Macsen) has a dream about a beautiful woman. He falls ill from lovesickness and sends messengers all over the world to determine her identity. He is only cured when his envoys discover who she is: Elen, the daughter of the king of Britain. Macsen travels to Britain and marries Elen. Later, her brothers help him reclaim Rome from usurpers. Macsen builds the Sarn Elen, a network of Roman roads through Wales, as a wedding present for his bride.

Scenes from Lug's childhood by Irish revolutionary and artist Maud Gonne, 1909: Lug in the Otherworld (left) and Manannán mac Lir giving a sword to Lug (right).

In a similar story from medieval Ireland, Óengus (another name for the Mac Óc whom we met earlier) dreams repeatedly of a beautiful woman named Caer, who plays music for him. He too falls into a listless, lovesick state, which lasts for a year. Many members of the Túatha Dé, hoping to cure Óengus, help search for the mysterious woman and eventually her identity is discovered. Caer's father tells Óengus that he does not have the ability to give his daughter away, as she is more powerful than her father and spends every other year in the form of a swan. Óengus eventually identifies her in her swan form and the two are united.

Music carried strong magical potential and was often linked to magical sleep. In one medieval Irish story, a talented harper sends courts and armies into an enchanted sleep with his music. This allows the hero of the tale to elope with his beloved and defeat his enemies. In the tale *Cath Maige Tuired* ('The Second Battle of Moytura') Lug also plays sleep-inducing music and the Dagda possesses a magical harp. The rival Fomorians steal this harp, but are unable to play it because the Dagda has bound the melodies inside of the instrument so that it remains silent. The Dagda eventually breaks into the hall where the harp is imprisoned and he magically calls it back to him by its two names, Daur Dá Bláo and Cóir Cetharchair:

Come Daur Dá Bláo,
Come Cóir Cetharchair,
Come summer, come winter,
Mouths of harps and bags and pipes!

The harp kills nine of its captors as it flies through the room into the Dagda's hands. The Dagda then plays three kinds of magical music in sequence: sorrowful, joyful and finally sleep-inducing. The sorrowful music causes the women to weep, the joyful music causes the women and boys to laugh and (predictably) the sleep-inducing music puts everyone into a slumber so that the Dagda can escape.

DRUIDS, PROPHETS AND POETS

As we have already seen, druids were favourite magical figures in the Lives of medieval Irish saints. They also populated vernacular literature set (but not written) in the pre-Christian past. Like the druids in Greek and Roman ethnography in Chapter 3 and the demonic adversaries whom St Patrick defeats in the hagiography in Chapter 4, these literary druids do not necessarily tell us much about real-life druids. But they are certainly exciting! Their powers and morals vary dramatically between accounts. One druid named Mog Ruith (literally, 'Slave of the Wheel') was said to have trained with the Biblical magician Simon Magus, against whom the apostle Peter contends in Acts 8:9–24. Mog Ruith was supposedly so evil and devoted to black magic that one medieval Irish poem claims that he even volunteered to execute John the Baptist. In another tale, however, Mog Ruith is more helpful and uses his magic arts to help the king of Munster defeat an invading army. Similarly, in many stories the druid Cathbad acts as magical advisor to the pre-Christian king of Ulster (for both good and ill), but in some narratives he also prophesies the crucifixion of Christ.

These stories of and attitudes towards magical behaviour vary so widely because, just like today, different authors had different ideas about magic and magicians, and different reasons for writing about them. Some authors depicted druids as evil sorcerers so that they could serve as dramatic antagonists for triumphant saints. Other authors instead used the helpful or prophetic druids of the pre-Christian past to show that God's grace had extended even to people who were not yet Christian, like the pagan ancestors of the medieval Irish. The idea that divine grace was at work in the world before the life of Christ was integral to how medieval Christian authors and audiences understood history. Medieval Christian writers argued that just as Old Testament kings and prophets had experienced divine grace despite living long before Christ, so too had their own forbears.

Queen Medb looks unimpressed at her druid's prophecy in an illustration by Stephen Reid for Eleanor Hull's *The Boys' Cuchulain*, 1904.

Prophecy was an important application of magic in medieval literature. In *Táin Bó Cúailnge*, a woman named Fedelm appears to Queen Medb to tell her that her expedition will end in disaster. When Medb asks about the fate of her army, Fedelm ominously predicts: 'I see it blood-stained, I see it red'. The line between prophet and poet was often a blurred one in both Irish and Welsh literature. In the *Táin*, Fedelm is both a prophet and a poet. Prophetic characters, including druids like Cathbad, often speak their prophecies in verse. In Welsh literature, poetic inspiration, known as *awen*, was often depicted as a divine or magical gift. Legendary poets such as Taliesin and Myrddin (the latter better known in English as Merlin) were said to possess *awen* and later medieval poets often appealed to *awen* to inspire their poetry.

Queen Medb in a romanticized depiction by Joseph Christian Leyendecker for T. W. Rolleston's *Myths and Legends of the Celtic Race*, 1911.

Magicians feature prominently in medieval Welsh tales. Merlin, whom we met in the introduction, may be the best known of these characters today, but he was hardly the only one. In the *Second Branch of the Mabinogi*, a magical cauldron restores the dead to life. In the *Third Branch of the Mabinogi*, a castle magically appears and disappears and a lord transforms his court into mice to eat the grain in his rival's fields. In the *Fourth Branch of the Mabinogi*, Math, the ruler of Gwynedd in northwest Wales, has a magic wand with which he can turn people into animals and discern a person's virginity. Despite Math's great powers, whenever he is not at war he must rest his feet in the lap of a virgin in order to survive. Math's nephew Gwydion is also a magician and uses his magic to start a war with neighbouring Dyfed in southwest Wales in order to distract Math while his brother Gilfaethwy rapes Math's virgin foot-bearer, Goewin. Upon Math's return, Goewin quickly tells him what has happened and Math punishes Gwydion and Gilfaethwy by turning them into various animals. Each year for three years they change species and sexes and have animal offspring until Math decides they have been suitably punished for their crimes. Math does the decent thing and marries Goewin to provide her with compensation and security, and sets out to find a new virgin foot-bearer.

Math's niece Arianrhod is the next candidate for virgin foot-bearer but she fails the virginity test: when she steps over Math's magic wand, she immediately gives birth to one child who runs away to live in the sea and to another, a premature lump of flesh that Gwydion keeps in a chest until it has finished gestating. Arianrhod abandons both children in shame and anger and Gwydion is left to raise the lump-of-flesh-turned-child as his own. When this child is grown, he is called Lleu. Because Arianrhod has cursed Lleu to never have a human wife, Math and Gwydion (who seem to have reconciled their differences at this point) join magical forces to create a woman out of flowers for Lleu to marry. The woman, named Blodeuwedd (literally,

A painting of Blodeuwedd by Christopher Williams, 1930. In the *Fourth Branch of the Mabinogi,* Blodeuwedd was created from flowers and magic.

Taliesin

Taliesin was a legendary Welsh poet who, over the course of the Middle Ages, increasingly became associated with magic. In the earliest written accounts that mention Taliesin, he was a court poet who wrote praise poetry for rulers of the distant past. Poetry is often linked with magical utterance, and in later medieval traditions, Taliesin became a magician and seer who was able to shapeshift and predict the future. In this excerpt from a later medieval poem called *Kat Godeu* ('The Battle of the Trees'), Taliesin introduces himself, listing the many forms he has had in the past:

I was a droplet in the air,
I was the stellar radiance of the stars.
I was a word in writing,
I was a book in my prime....

'Flower Face'), is not particularly happy about her arranged marriage and she plots with her lover Gronw Pebr to murder Lleu. Lleu survives the attempted murder but turns into an eagle and flies away. Gwydion must track him down and turn him back into a person. When Gwydion finds Lleu perched in a tree, he persuades him to come down by singing a series of verses known as *englynion*. The final stanza convinces Lleu to come down from the tree:

An oak grows on a slope
The refuge of a handsome prince.
Unless I am mistaken
Lleu will come to my lap.

(You can give this a try if you ever suspect a friend has been turned into a bird.) Lleu eventually recovers under Gwydion's care and gets his revenge on Gronw Pebr. At the end of the tale, Gwydion turns Blodeuwedd into an owl as punishment for her betrayal.

WITCHES AND BATTLE SPIRITS

Medieval literature in Celtic languages also features darker magical beings, including demonic battle spirits and witches. Irish works describe a range of sinister spirits that scream above the battlefield and feast on the dead afterwards. These are often bird-like creatures such as *badb* (translated as 'scald-crow'), probably because in reality ravens and crows tend to feed on carrion. One of the most prominent characters associated with bloody conflict is the Morrígan (literally, 'Great Queen'), a powerful Irish being who sometimes appears as a woman and sometimes as a hungry raven. In medieval literature and later stories and folklore, the Morrígan and related characters can be found washing the weapons and dismembered limbs of those about to die in battle. A warrior who came across one of these supernatural women washing his weapons knew that he was unlikely to survive his next combat. In a 14th-century Irish text, Richard de Clare, the head of a Hiberno-Norman family trying to conquer northern Munster, encounters one such woman, who ominously invites him and his entourage to hell. He ignores her warning at his own peril and is soon defeated by the local Irish ruler. Upon hearing the news of de Clare's death in battle, his wife burns their castle and flees back to England. We can only imagine the *badb*'s laughter echoing over the waves after her.

In an Old Irish poem called *Reicne Fothaid Canainne* ('The Poem of Fothad Canainne'), the ghost of a recently slain warrior appears to his lover and delivers a chilling warning:

> *Do not wait for the terror of night*
> *on the battle-field among the resting-places of the hosts;*
> *one should not converse with a dead man,*
> *go to your house, carry my spoils with you!*
> *... horrible are the huge entrails*

which the Morrígan washes.
She has come to us from the edge of a pillar,
it is she who has egged us on;
many are the spoils she washes,
horrible the hateful laugh she laughs.

The Morrígan also has prophetic knowledge and in one text she predicts the end of the world. Some aspects of the Morrígan and similar figures may in fact be pre-Christian survivals, others are inspired by medieval Christian traditions about demons, and still others show the influence of authors who were well-versed in Greco-Roman mythology. For example, in one version of *Táin Bó Cúailnge*, the classical Fury Allecto (known from the works of classical authors like Virgil) makes a brief appearance and causes chaos. In the manuscript, a scribe has helpfully provided a gloss on Allecto, explaining that this malevolent classical being is in fact the same character as the Morrígan. The mention of a classical Fury in a medieval text set in ancient Ireland is a learned allusion and reflects the monastic author's engagement with high levels of Latin literary culture. It may tell us more about what people were reading in the monastery than what everyday people actually thought about demons, battle spirits and supernatural women.

Irish battle spirits like the Morrígan often took the form of ravens and carrion crows.

In addition to Otherworldly beings like the Morrígan, mortal women who practise magic (and sometimes end up paying for it) also turn up in literary texts from across the Celtic-speaking world. We may call these women 'witches', although there are many words for such figures in Irish and Welsh, and they do not necessarily map exactly onto the connotations of the word 'witch' in modern English. In the medieval Welsh romance *Peredur vab Efrawc* ('Peredur son of Efrog'), Peredur, one of King Arthur's knights, confronts nine such supernatural women or 'witches' of Caer Loyw (modern-day Gloucester) who have been destroying a noblewoman's land and killing her people. The witches relent and teach Peredur useful knightly skills like riding and fighting. At the end of the tale, Peredur learns that the witches were responsible for beheading his cousin and injuring his uncle. Peredur and Arthur confront the witches once more and Peredur offers them several chances to cease their violent ways. However, they continue to kill Arthur's men in front of Peredur and the knight finally draws his sword. The leader of the witches reveals to her sisters (and the audience) that Peredur is the one destined to slay them and orders them to flee. Peredur and Arthur's other knights then attack and kill all the witches.

Several Irish tales tell how the legendary hero Conall Corc (literally, 'Red Conall') got his nickname from a characteristic red birthmark inflicted by supernatural women. As a child, Conall is fostered with a witch named Fedelm (this is a different Fedelm to the one who prophesies in *Táin Bó Cúailnge*). Some of Fedelm's sorcerous associates do not take kindly to the child and turn up at Fedelm's house one night with evil intent. Fedelm hides Conall in the ground under the hearth. The witches come into the house and one states that she does not harm anything except that which is under the cauldron. This causes the fire in the hearth to burn Conall on the ear, leaving a red mark from which he gets the nickname 'Corc' (which means red in Irish).

In this story, the witches walk about at night and have the power to control the fire in the hearth. Like druids in medieval Irish literature, these supernatural women are not all evil, however, as Fedelm herself is Conall's foster-mother and tries her best to protect him. Like the witches in *Peredur vab Efrawc*, these women are by turns nurturing and dangerous. Other witches with a propensity for violence appear in an early 13th-century text called the *Acallam na Senórach* ('The Tales of the Elders') in which St Patrick must defeat nine supernatural women who have been killing all of the inhabitants of an area, adults and children alike. People who were concerned about supernatural women like these could recite St Patrick's *lorica*, which offered protection against a range of natural and supernatural forces, including 'the spells of women and smiths and druids'.

The first witch trial in Ireland was held in 1324, well after most of the texts discussed in this book were written. The woman in question was a wealthy widow named Dame Alice Kyteler, whose four husbands had all perished in somewhat suspicious circumstances. Her accusers were the Bishop of Ossory and her stepchildren, who clearly had financial motives for wanting her out of the way. Among other things, Kyteler was accused of having sex with an incubus (a type of seductive male demon) to whom she also sacrificed animals; denying the power of Christ; lighting candles in the church at night; brewing potions from various human and animal body parts; and (predictably) ensnaring and killing her husbands through occult means. Whether any of these activities actually reflected real magical practices performed by anyone in medieval Ireland is unclear (but probably unlikely). Kyteler eventually fled the country but her servant Petronilla of Meath was not so lucky and was burned at the stake for witchcraft.

Witchcraft was a fairly minor legal misdemeanour in most of Europe up until the 14th century, when it was reclassified as a form of heresy by Pope John XXII. This allowed it to be tried by the Inquisition and it began to be treated as a more serious crime

A charm for ale

In one medieval Irish tale, a character named Athairne utters a charm that causes all the containers of ale in the house to burst open. The next time you think your pub landlord or host is being stingy with the ale give Athairne's charm a try, but be prepared for a bit of a mess in the process:

> *For ale, light of earth, waves of the ocean quickly surround land. An ocean which recedes, location of light, with a boundary breaking, a woman of fire. The hoops [of their barrels] burst, a nut breaking.*

The text reminds the reader that it is not proper to leave ale behind without drinking it. If the charm works for you, make sure the ale doesn't go to waste!

throughout Europe in the later Middle Ages and into the Early Modern period. Scotland saw a rash of witch trials between the 16th and the mid-18th centuries, especially after King James VI and I became convinced that a group of witches had tried to sink his ship at sea by raising violent storms in 1589. James's fascination with witchcraft is reflected by the trio of Scottish witches who appear in Shakespeare's tragedy *Macbeth*, initially performed in 1606 while James was on the throne. The first witch trial in Wales occurred in the 16th century but witch hunting in Wales never gained much traction; even when they did occur, most Welsh witchcraft trials ended in acquittal.

MAGICAL WRITING SYSTEMS?

In addition to the Latin alphabet, sometimes the Irish language was written in ogam (also spelled *ogham* in modern Irish), an alphabet that consisted of letters formed from individual hash-marks or dots connected to a central stemline. It was probably designed in the very early Middle Ages to be carved on wood or stone – in medieval manuscripts, many ogam letters are given names associated with trees or wood, which probably reflect the script's epigraphic origins. Some of these names might have been associated with specific ogam letters from an early date, while others may be later medieval inventions. Our earliest surviving examples of the Irish language are short ogam inscriptions on stones from the 5th and 6th centuries CE. Most of these early inscriptions record people's names and served as gravestones or property markers. It is unclear what (if any) mystical significance this writing system originally held; ogam was almost certainly invented by people familiar with the Latin alphabet and many of these inscriptions can be found near early church sites so we should probably think of them as part of an ecclesiastical context rather than a relic of the pagan past.

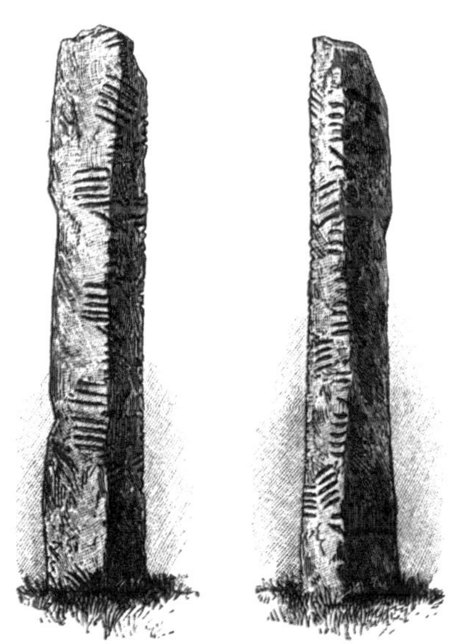

An antiquarian's drawing of weathered ogam stones.
Note the cross carved at the top of the stone on the right.

Several centuries later, however, medieval authors came up with their own ideas about ogam, magic and the pre-Christian past. One medieval text aptly entitled *In Lebor Ogaim* ('The Book of Ogam'), which circulated in several manuscripts, contains more than a hundred different types and uses of ogam including 'dog ogam', 'cow ogam' and even 'the secret ogam of warriors'. Runes used by Old Norse speakers are listed as 'Scandinavian ogam'. These variations on ogam and other special alphabets represented medieval writers' love of puzzles and cryptography and most probably never saw use outside of manuscripts. Clever scribes could encode their messages through letter substitution codes or by using different alphabets.

Some of the alphabets in *In Lebor Ogaim* also have divinatory potential. One, entitled 'boy ogam', allegedly allowed the user to determine the gender of an unborn child. The letters of the mother's name were counted and if they added up to an odd number, the child would be a boy; if they produced an even number, the child would be a girl. If the mother had already had a child, then you were supposed to use the letters in that child's name instead. It is unclear what you were supposed to do if the mother has already had multiple children. The underlying idea is reminiscent of children's games that involve tearing the petals off a flower in order to produce a Yes or No answer to a question (often involving the romantic affections of a potential love interest).

In Lebor Ogaim claims that the ogam alphabet was invented by Ogma, a member of the Túatha Dé:

> Now Ogma, a man well skilled in speech and poetry, invented the ogam. The cause of its invention, as a proof of his ingenuity, and that this speech should belong to the learned apart, to the exclusion of rustics and herdsmen.

This imagined origin for ogam mirrored the exclusivity of literacy in early medieval Ireland, which was largely restricted to the

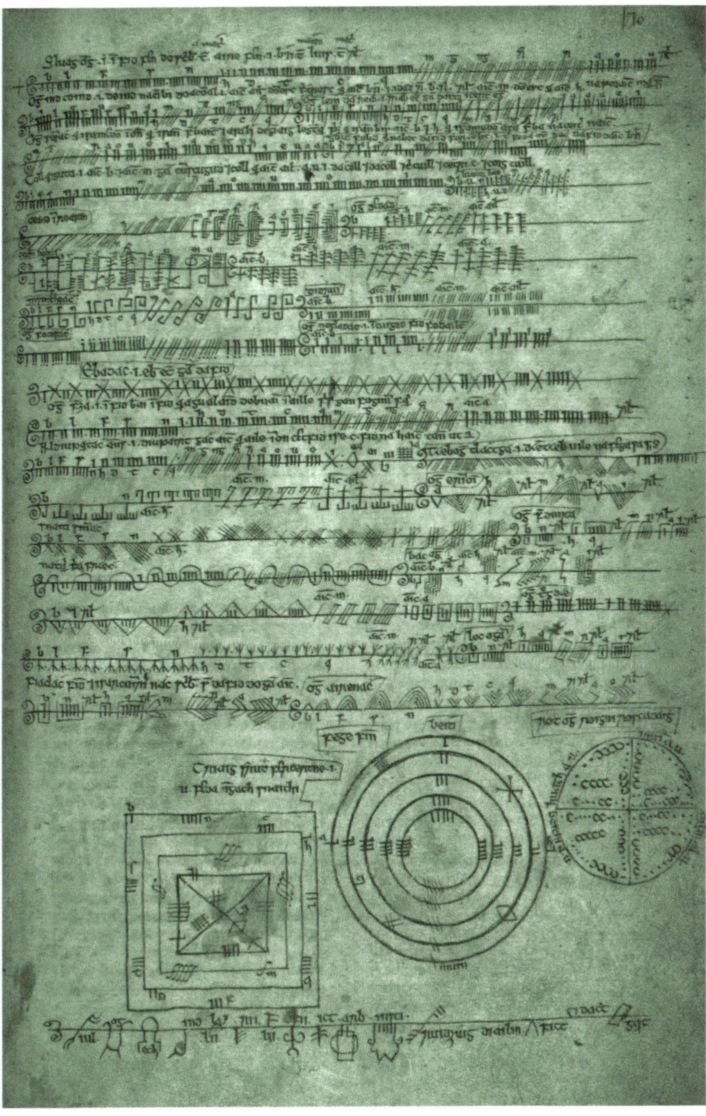

Some of the cryptic alphabets from *In Lebor Ogaim*, preserved in the Book of Ballymote in the collection of the Royal Irish Academy.

Learn the ogam alphabet

You can start learning the ogam alphabet with the most common version, found carved on stones and written in medieval manuscripts. Letters that appear below the horizontal stemline (b, l, f, s, n) can also appear to the right of a vertical stemline; letters that appear above a horizontal stemline (h, d, t, c, q) can also appear to the left on a vertical line.

ᚁ	ᚂ	ᚃ	ᚄ	ᚅ
b	l	f	s	n
ᚆ	ᚇ	ᚈ	ᚉ	ᚊ
h	d	t	c	q
ᚋ	ᚌ	ᚍ	ᚎ	ᚏ
m	g	ng	z	r
ᚐ	ᚑ	ᚒ	ᚓ	ᚔ
a	o	u	e	i

Can you work out what is written here?

clerically trained social elites. In this respect, ogam and the literacy it represented constituted a type of secret knowledge. However, this was privileged knowledge born of elite education and clerical learning rather than any occult pre-Christian survival.

The many variants of the ogam alphabet found in medieval Irish manuscripts are similar to the use of Greek, Hebrew, or other unfamiliar languages as learned, mystical gibberish, as we encountered in the previous chapter. Comparable elaborate invented writing systems could be found across the medieval world. A 9th-century manuscript from Britain contains an alphabet attributed to the Welsh monk Nennius. Nennius allegedly invented it after an English acquaintance mocked the Welsh for lacking their own alphabet comparable to the Old English or Old Norse runes. Like some of the complicated ogam variations in *In Lebor Ogaim*, the alphabet of Nennius was probably never used outside of a few manuscripts.

The desire to create secret Celtic-inspired alphabets continued long after the Middle Ages: the famed Welsh antiquarian and forger Iolo Morganwg invented his own rune-like alphabet called *Coelbren y Beirdd* ('The Alphabet of the Bards') in the late 18th century. In *The White Goddess* (originally published in 1948), the poet and novelist Robert Graves reinterpreted the ogam alphabet as an ancient calendar in which the (medieval) arboreal names of each ogam letter corresponded to specific lunar months. Graves went a step further, linking his fabricated calendar to several medieval Irish literary works, the medieval Welsh poem *Kat Godeu* (where we met Taliesin and some of his past forms), a baffling array of ancient Mediterranean imagery and imagined rituals of human sacrifice. This 'Celtic Tree Calendar' proved popular with some modern audiences but has no factual basis in the time-keeping or ritual practices of any known society of the past. However, this and many other types of Celtic-inspired ritual have been adapted and reinvented to suit the interests and needs of modern practitioners of magic.

Depictions of magic and magicians in medieval literature were rich and varied. Everyday landscape features might open onto wondrous Otherworldly dwellings. Druids could be evil antagonists for saints to defeat or examples of divine grace. Poets predicted the future, created life and sometimes shapeshifted into new forms. Throughout this diverse literary corpus, words had power. Whether it took the form of curses, charms, prophecies, secret alphabets or fabulous tales, language itself was magical.

AFTERLIVES

Magic and rituals practised by Celtic speakers in the past have had many afterlives since the Middle Ages. While interest in Celtic languages, literatures and belief systems never entirely evaporated, it reached new heights during the 18th and 19th centuries. Across Europe, authors and audiences inspired by Romanticism sought new (or adapted old) mythologies and histories to replace and augment the dominant ideas of the Age of Enlightenment. It was this era that popularized a link between Stonehenge and Celtic druids, promoted the medieval past as an alternative to rationalist modernity and saw the emergence of modern historical linguistics, a discipline that recognized that Celtic languages were related not only to one another, but also to the larger Indo-European language family, stretching from Ireland to the Indian subcontinent. These developments went hand-in-hand with the expansion of European colonialism and imperialism around the globe, and with developing nationalist sentiment throughout Europe and in the historically Celtic-speaking areas of Ireland, Wales, Scotland, Brittany, Cornwall and the Isle of Man.

By the later 19th century, twining strands of Romanticism and nationalism twisted together to form a group of cultural and political movements, which historians and literary scholars often refer to as the Celtic Revival. Among a range of diverse and sometimes contradictory goals, various strands of Celtic Revivalism promoted language revitalization, renewed interest in ancient and medieval literature and art, and in some cases (especially in Ireland) advocated for political self-rule. Front and centre in many Romantic and Revivalist discussions were the pre-Christian past, the medieval church and ideas about Celtic myth and magic.

ROMANTICISM AND NATIONALISM

Perhaps the most famous example of early Romantic interest in Celtic speakers of the distant past is James Macpherson's *Poems of Ossian*. Published in several volumes between 1761 and 1765, these works purported to be the ancient history of the hero Fingal that had been struck into verse by the 3rd-century CE poet Ossian, which Macpherson had collected from oral traditions in the Scottish Highlands and translated into English prose. The only problem was that the poems were almost entirely the fictitious inventions of Macpherson. Real medieval texts and early modern folklore about Finn mac Cumail (Finn MacCool) and his son Oisín lurk somewhere behind Macpherson's phony epic but modern scholars accept that his works were, at best, not entirely what they claimed to be and, at worst, wholesale forgeries.

Audiences immediately compared Ossian to the ancient Greek poet Homer and Macpherson's work was hailed as a sort of *Iliad* for Scotland (although Macpherson was met with plenty of sceptical detractors as well). *Ossian* was influential not only on emerging Romantic literary tastes but also on the way in which people viewed and responded to the Celtic past. Macpherson's opus is a poignant portrayal of a lost heroic world populated by the noble yet barbarous ancestors of the modern Scots (sometimes with dubiously Celtic names). Macpherson depicts relatively little magic or supernatural occurrences, all things considered, but this did not stop other writers from adding these to their own *Ossian*-inspired works.

Another Scottish author, Sir Walter Scott, captured both Romantic spirit and burgeoning nationalism with an occult flair in his poem 'The Bard's Incantation' (1804). In the lines excerpted here, a wandering bard conjures lost poets and heroes from the dead to fight again for Scotland:

Idealized visions of the Scottish past from an edition of James Macpherson's *Poems of Ossian*. Many of Macpherson's characters look more like Greco-Roman heroes than 3rd-century Celtic speakers.

There is a voice among the trees,
That mingles with the groaning oak –
That mingles with the stormy breeze,
And the lake-waves dashing against the rock; –
There is a voice within the wood,
The voice of the Bard in fitful mood;
His song was louder than the blast,
As the Bard of Glenmore through the forest past.
'Wake ye from your sleep of death,
Minstrels and bards of other days!
For the midnight wind is on the heath,
And the midnight meteors dimly blaze:
The Spectre with the Bloody Hand,
Is wandering through the wild woodland;
The owl and the raven are mute for dread,
And the time is meet to awake the dead!'

The gloomy atmospherics and spectral sights give way to a catalogue of Scottish victories (and some defeats) and the poem closes with the promise that these heroic deeds will inspire further pursuit of the 'joys of liberty'.

A somewhat muddled definition of Celticness is characteristic of 18th- and 19th-century Romantic poetry like that of Scott or Macpherson, even when it contains a clear vein of nationalism. It is as if the authors were not entirely sure which Celtic speakers they intended to depict. The poem quoted here does not distinguish the various Celtic-speaking inhabitants of Britain: medieval Irish settlers (the *Scotti,* who provided the namesake of Scotland) are to be found besides pre-Roman Britons and even 'Gaul's ravening legions'. English, French, Scottish, Welsh, Irish, Cornish and Breton authors, both Protestant and Catholic, could all lay claim to an amorphous and ill-defined 'Celtic' past to achieve their own ends.

Sir Walter Scott (1771–1832) was second only to Macpherson for popularizing a Romantic ideal of the ancient Celts.

Later works of Celtic-inspired Romanticism included Felix Mendelssohn's symphonic overture *The Hebrides* (1830–32), also known as *Fingal's Cave* after a sea cave on the Isle of Staffa named for Macpherson's fictional Fingal, and Vincenzo Bellini's opera *Norma* (1831). Both take as their subjects dramatic features of the vaguely Celtic past (the sea cave and Fingal in Mendelssohn's case and the bloodthirsty druids of Gaul in Bellini's opera). Neither composer had a personal nationalist connection to Britain, Ireland or Gaul/France, but their works show how widespread popular 'Celtomania' became throughout Europe by the mid-19th century.

IOLO MORGANWG AND THE DRUIDS

In Wales, antiquarian sentiment had been alive and well since at least the 16th century. Notorious Elizabethan occultist and Welshman John Dee is known to have collected several copies of Geoffrey of Monmouth's *History of the Kings of Britain*, including at least one version of its medieval translation into Welsh. However, for our purposes, the person who proved most influential for subsequent ideas about the religious practices of the ancient Britons and Welsh was Edward Williams, better known as Iolo Morganwg (Iolo of Glanmorgan) (d. 1826).

Born near Llancarfan, Vale of Glamorgan in 1747, Iolo Morganwg had a prolific career as a stonemason, author, editor, collector of manuscripts, forger and leader of a secret society. The society in question was *Gorsedd Beirdd Ynys Prydain* (The Gorsedd of the Bards of the Island of Britain) and with it Iolo sought to resurrect what he believed to be the ancient gorsedd or meeting of the bardic poets of Britain. Originally, the medieval Welsh word *gorsedd* meant 'hill' or 'mound' (the second component, *-sedd*, is related to the Irish word *síd*), but in medieval texts it could refer to a legal court or a meeting as well because such gatherings were often held on hills or mounds. Not content to link his reborn Gorsedd with medieval poets and princes alone, Iolo traced its origins to the pre-Christian druids of Britain, whom he claimed had themselves learned their beliefs and rituals from Old Testament patriarchs. Like the later Gaelic Revival authors in Ireland, Iolo compared some of these beliefs to Hinduism, especially druidic doctrines of reincarnation. Iolo believed that ancient Druidry was not only compatible with Christianity but that it had represented a better, truer form of the faith before it was corrupted by later monarchs and churches (read, the English and the Catholic Church, among others).

Iolo divided his Bardic order into Bards, Druids and Ovates (a term that originally derived from a misunderstanding of *Ovydd*,

Edward Williams (1747–1826), better known as Iolo Morganwg: author, collector, forger and founder of the modern Gorsedd.

the medieval Welsh name for the classical Latin poet Ovid). These divisions persist among some druidic groups today. Naturally, Iolo himself was the leader of the Gorsedd, which conducted various rituals throughout the year, including erecting stone circles, ritually unsheathing swords and reciting prayers and poetry.

Like James Macpherson, Iolo Morganwg was not above forging medieval sources when it suited his purposes. While some of his many publications do contain authentic medieval Welsh texts from the manuscripts that he collected, others were entirely his own invention and often served to shore up his theories about druids, philosophy and Welsh identity. One of Iolo's creative compositions, known as 'The Druid's Prayer' or 'The *Gorsedd's* Prayer', went through several iterations during his lifetime. The first version is presented here:

God, impart Thy strength;
And in strength, power to suffer;
And to suffer for the truth;
And in the truth, all light;
And in light, all happiness;
And in happiness, love;
And in love, God;
And in God, all goodness.

Another, altogether more cryptic poem for the winter solstice goes as follows:

When the country of Gwrthenin shall bewail a stratagem,
To the notches of rods shall the secluded populace repair;
Blessed the lips that shall easily, and in confidential
secrecy,
Pronounce three words of the ancient and primitive
language.

These three words and their magical significance were supposedly known only to the bards. Iolo attributes this poem to Merddin Emrys, one of the pseudo-historical medieval personages on whom Geoffrey of Monmouth based the magician Merlin.

The Gorsedd created by Iolo Morganwg in 1798 still exists today as *Gorsedd Cymru* (the Gorsedd of Wales), an organization dedicated to honouring and promoting Welsh language, literature, music and culture. Since the mid-20th century, it has distanced itself from claims of druidic or mythological origins. An Archdruid (*Archdderwydd*) still leads the Gorsedd today but now primarily serves as a cultural ambassador and performs duties that include presiding over the *Eisteddfod Genedlaethol Cymru* (the National *Eisteddfodd* of Wales), an important annual Welsh-language festival and music and poetry competition.

TRANSLATORS AND TRANSLATION

While classical Greco-Roman ideas about ancient Celtic speakers were available to any educated reader of Latin and Greek (and often in English translations for everyone else), few Romantic authors and artists from Anglophone backgrounds could access texts in their original medieval Welsh and Irish languages. Two aristocratic women changed this and in so doing were instrumental in establishing a canon of medieval Welsh and Irish literature.

Lady Charlotte Guest (d. 1895) translated a collection of medieval Welsh prose texts collectively entitled the *Mabinogion* (after the *Four Branches of the Mabinogi*, which forms a part – but not all – of the collection). While most of these texts can be found together in the same medieval manuscripts, their contents and style are varied. They include the *Four Branches*, as well as Arthurian Romances in Welsh like *Peredur*, and other stand-alone tales, such as *Breuddwyd Macsen* (all of which are mentioned in the previous chapter). Guest was not Welsh herself, but she quickly learned the language after marrying a Welsh engineer and moving to Dowlais in Merthyr Tydfil, southern Wales. For nearly a century, Guest's translation of the *Mabinogion* texts remained the only one available in English.

Lady Augusta Gregory (d. 1932) provided a similar service for medieval Irish literature. She was born into an aristocratic

Lady Charlotte Guest (1812–1895), translator of the medieval Welsh *Mabinogion* texts.

Anglo-Irish family in County Galway and learned Irish as a child. Lady Gregory published several collections of English translations based on medieval Irish material, including, most famously, *Cuchulain of Muirthemne* (1902) and *Gods and Fighting Men* (1904). Some of these translations are near-literal renderings of medieval texts, while others have been embellished or stitched together to produce cohesive narratives out of disparate medieval sources. Unlike Guest, Gregory presented what had originally been separate texts as single, interconnected narratives, giving the impression

Lady Augusta Gregory (1852–1932), known for her theatrical works and (fairly loose) translations of medieval Irish literature.

that medieval Irish literature possessed far greater cohesion than it originally had. Gregory was also a folklore collector, playwright and patron of other Gaelic Revival authors including W. B. Yeats and George Russell (better known as 'Æ').

MYSTICISM AND CELTIC REVIVALS

In 1890, Oscar Wilde's mother confidently stated that 'All nations and races from the earliest time have held the intuitive belief that mystic beings were always all around them', much as the Roman historian Pliny the Elder had once claimed (as we saw earlier) that 'People across the whole world are similar in this way, although they are separate and ignorant of one another'. Where Pliny's statement was dismissive, however, lumping British and Persian magic together as a continuum of superstition, Lady Jane Wilde celebrated what she saw to be the shared mystical experience of humanity. She even went so far as to propose that pre-Christian Irish druids worshipped the ancient Phoenician/Canaanite deities Baal and Ashtaroth.

Just as Greco-Roman authors like Pliny could be quick to link the magic and religions of Celtic speakers to those of peoples living

Maud Gonne (1866–1953) provided illustrations for the children's book *The Coming of Lug*, inspired by characters from medieval Irish literature.

Portrait of George Russell ('Æ') (1867–1935) by his friend and colleague William Butler Yeats (1865–1939).

east of the Mediterranean, so too did authors and spiritualists of the later 19th and early 20th centuries associated with Celtic (and especially Gaelic) Revival movements. Gaelic Revival literati W. B. Yeats and George Russell sought to blend Irish pre-Christian beliefs with 'Eastern' religions, which included aspects of Buddhism and Hinduism among others. This created a new mishmash of universalized mysticism (and often perpetuated colonialist and Orientalist stereotypes in the process). Many of these Anglo-Irish writers relied on translations of medieval Irish (and Welsh) material penned by Augusta Gregory and Charlotte Guest.

In the late 1890s, Yeats, Russell and Maud Gonne (a revolutionary, artist and actress who was also a sometime love interest of Yeats) formed an occult group called the Order of Celtic Mysteries, inspired by other occultist organizations such as the Hermetic Order of the Golden Dawn, the theosophical doctrines propounded by the spiritualist Helena Blavatsky and what they believed to be ancient Irish mythology. A litany composed by members of the Order provides an example of the sorts of mystical liturgies practised by Yeats, Russell and others in their circle:

Aengus [Old Irish Óengus] chief of the young
we evoke thee
Master of the four winds we evoke thee
Guarder of Grainne we evoke thee
Sojourner with Midir we evoke thee
Sojourner in [the] Brugh we evoke thee
Lover of Fame we evoke thee.

Litanies like this one were intended to summon a vision of Aengus so that members of the Order could gain esoteric knowledge and spiritual understanding. There are some references to medieval literature and literary characters here (Aengus/Óengus, Grainne, Midir, the Brugh) mixed with new contributions (Master of the four winds, Lover of Fame). Does the fact that the members of the Celtic Mysteries invented this litany from scratch make it any more or less magical or effective than any of the earlier examples of magic that we have already encountered? The Order of Celtic Mysteries dissolved by 1902, but it was not the last or only attempt to meld occultism and mysticism with a romanticized idea of pre-Christian Celtic beliefs. This (imagined) Irish mythic past continued to influence the works of Yeats, Russell and their contemporaries for decades.

Maud Gonne gives Lug a crown of golden solar rays in one of her illustrations for Ella Young's *The Coming of Lug*.

The sea god Manannán mac Lir holds baby Lug in another of Maud Gonne's illustrations.

FAIRIES, FOLKLORE AND RACIAL SCIENCE

By the late 19th and early 20th centuries, writers such as Walter Evans-Wentz, author of *The Fairy-Faith in the Celtic Countries* (1911), felt that modern folklore from historically Celtic-speaking regions both perpetuated and could be used to reconstruct systems of pre-Christian Celtic belief. There is probably a grain of truth to some of these ideas: popular oral traditions and elite literary culture were not entirely separate spheres in the Middle Ages and oral traditions that might or might not have pre-dated Christianity probably found their way into some medieval texts. Likewise, medieval literary characters can certainly be found in folklore collected in the 19th century and today, either because they share a common, oral source or because medieval literature itself influenced later oral traditions. Just like medieval scribes, tellers of folklore reshape existing traditions and invent new tales as well, so we usually cannot know whether a certain tale or character represents direct continuity with the distant past.

Across Europe, various literary scholars, folklore collectors, early anthropologists and popular writers saw the fairies and sprites of folklore as survivals of pre-Christian gods and, in some cases, proof that paganism had never really died out during the Middle Ages but just gone underground. Some authors and anthropologists of the 19th and early 20th centuries also argued that the fairies of popular folklore represented generational memory of earlier races of humans (or not-quite-humans) who had once inhabited Britain and Ireland. The link between not-quite-humans and earlier (often implicitly lesser) races had roots in pseudo-historical narratives written in the Middle Ages about successive waves of invasion and migration, but it also drew from what was, for the time, cutting-edge science: Darwin's theory of evolution. The conceit that the fairies were echoes of earlier races that had since been replaced by the 'superior' race

A mystical painting by George Russell ('Æ') depicting the medieval Irish heroine Deirdre against a starry backdrop.

of modern humans thus represented the application of Darwinian evolution to racial science. Put simply, this was racism.

These racial attitudes were frequently coupled with classicism directed towards the rural and lower classes from whom folklore tended to be collected. Rural and lower-class interlocutors were by turns derided as uneducated country bumpkins and praised as 'noble savages' (much like Macpherson's Ossian), but in either case they were seen as the unthinking transmitters of ancient pagan ritual to the modern day (much as medieval scribes were once seen as unthinking copyists, transferring pre-Christian beliefs to parchment). The past was treated as a more 'primitive' (if sometimes more honest) time that could only be understood through comparisons with supposedly 'primitive' echelons of modern society (i.e. rural and lower-class people) or with non-Western societies deemed to be 'primitive' from colonial and imperialist perspectives. Not every early folklore collector or anthropologist thought this way, but it is important to realize that these kind of 'primitivist' ideas formed a major strand in the popularization and academic study of ancient Celtic (and other pre-Christian) belief systems in the 19th century, and continued into the 20th century.

The idea that the pagan beliefs of ancient Europe (Celtic and otherwise) had survived through the Middle Ages and perhaps lingered to the present day in rural backwaters and hidden ceremonies underpinned Margaret Murray's influential book *The Witch Cult in Western Europe* (1921). In *The Witch Cult* and its sequels, Murray advanced the theory that an ancient pagan witch cult had survived the Christianization of western Europe and (again) that the fairies of folklore were based on an ancient race of dwarves who had also lived into the historical period. Murray's witch cult has been roundly dismissed as fantasy by modern scholars but aspects of her theories influenced numerous other writers and thinkers of the 20th century, including Robert Graves and Gerald Gardner, one of the founders of Wicca (a popular modern pagan religion, sometimes also known simply as 'Witchcraft' or 'The Craft', that venerates two primary deities known as the Horned God and the Mother Goddess).

CELTIC MAGIC TODAY

People today continue to find meaning in beliefs inspired by Celtic speakers and Celtic literature of the past. These beliefs are as varied as the ancient and medieval sources that produced them and as diverse as their modern practitioners. There is no single 'right way' to practise Celtic magic today and different people draw from their personal experiences and take inspiration from both within and beyond the Celtic-speaking world. Many modern practitioners of Celtic-inspired magic practise individually or belong to relatively decentralized groups of fellow worshippers and have developed a panoply of unique traditions.

Haitian Vodou, for example, is an African diasporic religion that includes an important *loa* (or spirit) called Maman Brigitte. Maman Brigitte owes aspects of her identity to the Irish St Brigit in addition to religions brought to the Caribbean during the transatlantic trade in enslaved people, and indigenous Caribbean belief systems. Elements of this spirit also reflect the worship of the Virgin Mary and Mary Magdalene. Maman Brigitte is usually said to be the consort of Baron Samedi, a *loa* associated with death, and is often portrayed with a black rooster. People sometimes make her offerings of alcohol and spicy food. The influences at work in the complex syncretism of Vodou are varied and multiple, and represent the rich blending of beliefs that people have practised for millennia.

Around the world, modern pagan movements (often referred to as neopaganism) too numerous to list also draw on and reshape beliefs associated with ancient and medieval Celtic speakers. The Horned God of Wicca (and related belief systems), is identified by some Wiccans and practitioners of modern paganism as the Gaulish deity Cernunnos. Celtic Reconstructionists try to base their worship on historically grounded practices of pre-Christian Celtic speakers, drawing on archaeological, literary and linguistic evidence to inform their ritual and practice. Other pagans prefer to merge Celtic-inspired elements with different belief systems and find further inspiration in Old Norse literature, ancient Mediterranean polytheism and other world religions. Some modern pagans emphasize learning ancient or modern Celtic languages and support language revitalization efforts for minority languages.

Many modern pagan groups divide the year into four quarters and celebrate the 'quarter days' that fall halfway between the solstices

St Brigit's crosses are often woven from reeds or grass to celebrate the saint's feast day on 1 February.

and the equinoxes by their Irish names: Samhain (1 November), Imbolc (1 February), Beltaine (1 May) and Lughnasadh (1 August). In Wicca, these holidays form part of the annual cycle of observances known as the Wheel of the Year. These days all appear in medieval Irish literature (as well as in folklore collected at a later date) as important dates in the agricultural and the Christian liturgical calendar. Samhain (1 November) is probably the best known of these holidays and appears often in medieval literature as a time when people can travel to the Otherworld with ease. In *Echtra Neraí* ('The Adventure of Nera'), the protagonist Nera goes on escapades with a reanimated corpse, travels to the Otherworld and sees a disastrous vision of the future on Samhain; he is able to return from the Otherworld in time to prevent calamity from occurring. In some tales, monsters appear on Samhain and must be defeated by heroes or saints. In *Acallam na Senórach* ('The Tales of the Elders'), St Patrick defeats a group of malicious werewolves who have been attacking livestock. Modern pagans often commemorate the spirits of the departed on Samhain and believe that the veil between the worlds of the living and the dead and between the Otherworld and the mortal world is thinner on this particular date. Some traditions associated with Samhain or with All Souls' and All Saints' Days (celebrated on 1 and 2 November in many liturgical calendars) ultimately influenced Halloween customs around the world.

Imbolc (also spelled Imbolg) falls on 1 February, a date shared with St Brigit's Day and Candlemas. One medieval Irish text, *Tochmarc Emire* ('The Wooing of Emer'), states that Imbolc marks the beginning of spring and the time when sheep can begin to be milked. Historically, people would celebrate St Brigit's day by making St Brigit's crosses and small figurines of the saint out of rushes and by leaving strips of cloth outside overnight for the saint to bless. Many of these folk traditions continue today and people of multiple faiths make St Brigit's crosses in order to feel connected to the Christian saint, the putative pre-Christian Irish goddess or to a sense of Irish or 'Celtic' identity. Some modern pagans symbolically extinguish and relight fires and candles on Imbolc to celebrate the return of longer days in the northern hemisphere.

Tochmarc Emire also states that Beltaine (1 May; sometimes also spelled Beltane) was the start of summer, when druids would build two large bonfires and drive their cattle between them in order to protect them from illness in the coming year. The association with fire and druids might owe less to actual memory of pre-Christian ritual and more to medieval etymologies that connected the name of the holiday with Bel or Baal, the god of the Canaanites in the Old Testament. In this regard, medieval Irish authors themselves were perhaps not so different from Lady Wilde and her attempts to link pre-Christian Celtic religion with better-known gods of the ancient Mediterranean. Modern pagans often link Beltaine with other May

Day festivities around the world, including Walpurgis Night, celebrations of the Virgin Mary and even International Workers' Day.

Lughnasadh (1 August) or Lammas was the date of the *Óenach Tailten* ('Fair of Tailtiu'), a celebration in medieval Irish literature that was held annually at Teltown, County Meath. *Tochmarc Emire* claims that the Otherworldly hero Lug established this celebration after the Battle of Moytura to celebrate the victory of the Túatha Dé over the Fomorians and his inauguration as king. In another Irish text, *Lebor Gabála Érenn* ('The Book of the Invasions of Ireland'), Lug set up the *Óenach Tailten* as a series of poetic and athletic competitions to honour the memory of his foster-mother Tailtiu. Various spiritual and secular attempts to revive the games associated with the *Óenach Tailten* have taken place since the 19th century. Some pagans today link Lughnasadh to the harvest and celebrate the abundance of the natural and agricultural world on this day.

The summer and winter solstices are also important for many practitioners of modern paganism. Self-declared pagans gather at Stonehenge and other prehistoric sites once associated with Celtic druids to watch the sun rise on the winter and summer solstices. Just as the religions and magical systems of the past were varied and diverse, so too are the goals and perspectives of modern worshippers multiple and sometimes conflicting. Vandalism of Stonehenge in 2024 by climate activists was met with both ideological solidarity and spiritual distress from practising pagans.

Contemporary interpretations of Celtic magic can represent equally meaningful spiritual experiences for their practitioners as creating curse tablets did for ancient Gaulish speakers or reciting *loricae* did for medieval Irish speakers. In some cases, scholars may point to a lack of continuity with Celtic religions of the past (especially pre-Christian belief systems), but this does not invalidate the spiritual experiences of modern believers. Most pagans today have eschewed the racial science and nationalist sentiments of earlier eras

Modern pagans celebrate the winter solstice at Stonehenge. The last century has seen recurrent arguments about conservation and the accessibility of Stonehenge to archaeologists, pagans and the general public.

(although racial prejudice is still an issue impacting some neopagan groups, as is the appropriation of indigenous belief systems around the world). Modern-day practitioners continue to incorporate elements from outside the Celtic-speaking world as well, syncretizing Celtic deities and beliefs with other traditions in a way ultimately akin to that of Roman Gaul or Britain or medieval Ireland and Wales.

Even if you follow the rituals and incantations in this book to the letter, your experience of them will differ from the experience of someone in 1st-century Gaul, Roman Bath, 8th-century Ireland, 13th-century Wales, Romantic-era Scotland or early 20th-century Dublin. It will also probably differ from another reader's experience of the same magic. While this guide has tracked trends in magical practice over time, magic remains a highly individual and personal activity. Go forth and may St Patrick defend you against every hostile, savage power and all knowledge which harms the soul.

NOTES AND FURTHER READING

Not all the sources that appear under 'Further Reading' entirely agree with each other or with what I have said in this book. As I hope is apparent from the introduction, both 'Celtic' and 'magic' are slippery and often inexact terms, and our surviving evidence for ancient and medieval Celtic-speaking people and places is imperfect. Different scholars have different views on this material and these views can change over time. I have tried to include a representative range of current academic thinking on ancient and medieval religions of Celtic speakers. Although I try to list the most up-to-date scholarly perspectives where possible, at some point these views too may be replaced with different arguments, especially as new evidence comes to light. Finally, while many of the sources I cite here are academic books or articles, I have tried to give references to online and popular sources as well for readers without access to academic library collections. If not otherwise attributed, translations are my own.

INTRODUCTION

Geoffrey of Monmouth's full narrative about Stonehenge: Reeve, Michael D. and Wright, Neil, *The History of the Kings of Britain: An Edition and Translation of the Britonum [Historia Regum Britanniae]* (Woodbridge, 2007), 171–75.

FURTHER READING

Merlin in medieval Welsh literature: see the Welsh Merlin Poetry project (https://myrddin.swansea.ac.uk/welcome/).

CHAPTER 1

Text and commentary on the Epona inscription: Hirschfeld, O. *et al.* (eds), *Corpus Inscriptionum Latinarum*, vol. 13, *Inscriptiones trium Galliarum et Germaniarum Latinae* (1899–1943), reference number 02902. **Ogmios and Hercules**: Lucian, *Hercules*, 1–6. **Text and commentary on more inscriptions from Gaul and Britain:** Lambert, Pierre-Yves, *La Langue Gauloise* (3rd edn, Paris, 1997); Lejeune, Michel *et al.*, *Recueil des inscriptions gauloises, XLVe supplément à Gallia* (Paris, 1985–2002), vols I, II.1, II.2, III, IV; Roman Inscriptions of Britain (https://romaninscriptionsofbritain.org/).

FURTHER READING

Celtic and Roman religions: Henig, Martin, *Religion in Roman Britain* (London, 1984); Jufer, Nicole and Luginbühl, Thierry, *Répertoire des dieux gaulois. Les noms des divinités celtiques connus par l'épigraphie, les textes antiques et la toponymie* (Paris, 2001); Koch, John (ed.), *Celtic Culture: A Historical Encyclopedia* (Santa Barbara, CA, 2006). **Images of the Pillar of the Boatmen and the finds from the sanctuary of Sequana:** see the websites of the Musée de Cluny and the Musée Archéologique de Dijon.

CHAPTER 2

Text, commentary and proposed translations for Bath Tabella 18: Proposed translation i: Schrijver, Peter, 'Early Celtic diphthongization and the Celtic-Latin interface', in J. de Hoz, E. R. Luján and P. Sims-Williams (eds), *New Approaches to Celtic Place Names in Ptolemy's Geography* (Madrid, 2005), 55–67. Proposed translation ii: Mullen, Alex, 'Evidence for Written Celtic from Roman Britain: A Linguistic Analysis of *Tabellae Sulis* 14 and 18', *Studia Celtica* 41 (2007), 31–45. Proposed translation iii: Mees, Bernard, *Celtic Curses* (Woodbridge, 2009), 29–49. **Text and commentary on the Chamalières and Larzac inscriptions:** Lambert, Pierre-Yves, *La Langue Gauloise* (3rd edn, Paris, 1997), 149–60; Mees, Bernard, *Celtic Curses* (Woodbridge, 2009), 10–28, 50–69; Lejeune, Michel *et al.*, *Recueil des inscriptions gauloises*, XLVe supplément à Gallia (Paris, 1985–2002), vols I, II.1, II.2, III, IV. **Text and commentary on the Latin curse tablets from Uley and Bath:** Tomlin, Roger S. O., 'The Latin Curses from Uley and Other Sanctuaries in Britain', *Religion in the Roman Empire* 7.1 (2021), 19–30; Tomlin, Roger S. O., 'Tabellae Sulis: Roman Inscribed Tablets of Tin and Lead from the Sacred Spring at Bath' in B. W. Cunliffe (ed.), *The Temple of Sulis Minerva at Bath II: The Finds from the Sacred Spring* (Oxford, 1988). **Text and commentary on the *defixiones* from Gallia Narbonensis, Trier and Bregenz:** Urbanová, Daniela, *Latin Curse Tablets of the Roman Empire* (Innsbruck, 2018), 82–83, 115, 301, 307–8.

FURTHER READING

Tolkien: Tolkien, J. R. R., 'The Name *Nodens*', *Tolkien Studies* 4.1 (2007), 177–83. **Multilingual communities in the Roman world:** Adams, J. N., *Bilingualism and the Latin Language* (Cambridge, 2003). **Curses in antiquity:** Gager, John G., *Curse Tablets and Binding Spells from the Ancient World* (Oxford, 1999). **Inscriptions from Roman Britain (including curses):** Inscriptions of Britain (https://romaninscriptionsofbritain.org/).

CHAPTER 3

Ancient sources: Julius Caesar, *Gallic Wars*, Book 6.11–20; Diodorus Siculus, *Bibliotheca Historica*, 5.27–32; Strabo, *Geography*, 4.4.4–6; Cicero, *De Divinatione*, 1.41.90; Lucan, *Bellum Civile*, 1.447–58; Athenaeus, *Deipnosophistae*, 4.160; Ammianus Marcellinus, *Res Gestae*, 15.9.8; Pomponius Mela, *De Situ Orbis*, 3.18–19, 48; Suetonius, *Claudius*, 25; Pliny the Elder, *Natural History*, 16.24, 29.52; Virgil, *Aeneid*, 4.512–14; Tacitus, *Annales*, 14.30; Ausonoius, *Commemoratio Professorum Burdigalensium*, 4, 10; *Historia Augusta*: Lampridius, *Alexander Severus*, 59.5, Vopiscus, *Numerianus*, 14 and *Aurelian*, 44. **For a wider variety of classical ethnography in translation:** Koch, John T. and Carey, John, *The Celtic Heroic Age* (4th edn, Aberystwyth, 2003); Freeman, Philip, *War, Women and Druids* (Austin, TX, 2002).

FURTHER READING

For more discussions of classical authors and ethnography about Celtic

speakers: Rankin, H. D., *The Celts and the Classical World* (London, 1987); Chapman, Malcolm, *The Celts: The Construction of a Myth* (Basingstoke, 1992); Riggsby, Andrew M., *Caesar in Gaul and Rome: War in Words* (Austin, TX, 2006); Hutton, Ronald, *Blood and Mistletoe: The History of the Druids in Britain* (London, 2009), ch. 1; Aldhouse-Green, Miranda, *Caesar's Druids: Story of an Ancient Priesthood* (London, 2010); Woolf, Greg, *Tales of the Barbarians: Ethnography and Empire in the Roman West* (Malden, MA, 2011); Gruen, Erich S., *Rethinking the Other in Antiquity* (Princeton, NJ, 2011), chs. 5 and 6.

CHAPTER 4

Translation of the *Life of St Cadog*: Wade-Evans, A. W. (ed.), *Vitae Sanctorum Britanniae et Genealogiae* (Cardiff, 1988), 113; more translations of Welsh saints' Lives can be found in this book and online at the University of Wales's Seintiau Project (https://saints.wales/). **Translation of the *Life of St Samson*:** Taylor, Thomas, *The Life of St Samson of Dol* (London, 1925). **Translation of *Buile Shuibhne*:** O'Keeffe, James G., *Buile Shuibhne* (Dublin, 1904), available online at the CELT [Corpus of Electronic Texts] database (https://celt.ucc.ie/published/T302018.html). **Translation of *St Patrick's Lorica*:** adapted from Todd, J. H., *St. Patrick, Apostle of Ireland: A Memoir of His Life and Mission* (Dublin, 1864), 426–29. **More of Tírechán and Muirchú's *Life of St Patrick*:** Bieler, Ludwig, *Patrician Texts in the Book of Armagh* (Dublin, 1979), also available online (https://confessio.ie/).

FURTHER READING

Relics in medieval Ireland: Wycherly, Niamh, *The Cult of Relics in Early Medieval Ireland* (Turnhout, 2016). **The *Beati* and medieval Irish religious literature:** Boyle, Elizabeth, *History and Salvation in Medieval Ireland* (Abingdon, 2021). ***Loricae* (and their relationships to the medical charms discussed in Chapter 5):** Tuomi, Ilona *et al.* (eds), *Charms, Charmers and Charming in Ireland: From the Medieval to the Modern* (Cardiff, 2019). **Apotropaic magic:** Borsje, Jacqueline, *The Celtic Evil Eye and Related Mythological Motifs in Medieval Ireland* (Leuven, 2012).

CHAPTER 5

Text and translation of the *Lorica* of Laidcenn/Gildas: adapted from Williams, Hugh, *Gildas, De excidio Britanniae, fragmenta, liber de paenitentia, accedit et Lorica Gildae* (London, 1899), 305–12. **Translation of the Old Irish hound charm:** Borsje, Jacqueline, 'A Spell Called *Éle*', in G. Toner and S. Mac Mathúna (eds), *Ulidia 3: Proceedings of the Third International Conference on the Ulster Cycle of Tales, University of Ulster, Coleraine 22–25 June, 2009: In Memoriam Patrick Leo Henry* (2013), 193–212. **Text and commentary on medieval Welsh recipes (including many more recipes):** Luft, Diana, *Medieval Welsh Medical Texts* (Cardiff, 2020), also available online (https://

www.ncbi.nlm.nih.gov/books/NBK558253/). **Text and commentary on the Old Irish headache and urinary infection charms:** Tuomi, Ilona, 'Parchment, Praxis and Performance of Charms in Early Medieval Ireland', *Incantatio* 3 (2013), 60–85; Tuomi, Ilona *et al.* (eds), *Charms, Charmers and Charming in Ireland: From the Medieval to the Modern* (Cardiff, 2019), ch. 4.

FURTHER READING

Medieval medicine in general: Hayden, Deborah and Baccianti, Sarah (eds), *Medicine in the Medieval North Atlantic World: Vernacular Texts and Traditions* (Turnhout, 2025), see ch. 17 by David Stifter for more Old Irish charms. **Old English in Old Irish charms:** Hayden, Deborah, 'Old English in the Irish Charms', *Speculum* 97.2 (2022), 349–76. **Medical comparisons from medieval England:** Batten, Caroline, *Health and the Body in Early Medieval England* (Cambridge, 2024). **Astrology in medieval Ireland and Wales:** Williams, Mark, *Fiery Shapes: Celestial Portents and Astrology in Ireland and Wales 650–1650* (Oxford, 2010).

CHAPTER 6

Translations of *Four Branches of the Mabinogi*: Davies, Sioned, *The Mabinogion* (Oxford, 2007), 62–63. **Translation from *Cath Maige Tuired*:** Gray, Elizabeth, *Cath Maige Tuired: The Second Battle of Mag Tuired* (Dublin, 1982). **Translation of *Kat Godeu*:** Haycock, Margred, *Legendary Poems from the Book of Taliesin* (Aberystwyth, 2007), 174–75. **Translation of *Reicne Fothaid Canainne*:** adapted from Meyer, Kuno, *Fianaigecht* (Dublin, 1910), 1–17. **Translations from *In Lebor Ogaim*:** adapted from Calder, George, *Auraicept na nÉces. The Scholars' Primer* (Edinburgh, 1917), 273. **For more translations of medieval texts:** Carey, John and Koch, John T., *The Celtic Heroic Age* (4th edn, Aberystwyth, 2003); Gantz, Jeffrey, *Irish Myths and Sagas* (Harmondsworth, 1981). **Full text of 'The Taking of the *Síd*':** Hull, Vernam, '*De gabáil in t-shída* (Concerning the seizure of the fairy mound)', *Zeitschrift* für *celtische Philologie* 19 (1933), 53–58. **An older text and a different translation of *Noínden Ulad*:** Henderson, George, *Leabhar nan Gleann: The Book of the Glens; with Zimmer on Pictish Matriachy (Edinburgh, 1898), 304–7,* also available online (https://iso.ucc.ie/Noinden-ulad/Noinden-ulad-text.html). **More discussion of the Irish banishing charm and of Aithairne's ale charm:** Carey, John, 'Charms in Medieval Irish Tales: Tradition, Adaptation, Invention', in Ilona Tuomi *et al.* (eds), *Charms, Charmers and Charming in Ireland: From the Medieval to the Modern* (Cardiff, 2019), 20–23. **Full text of *Conall Corc and the Corco Luigde:*** Hull, Vernam, 'Conall Corc and the Corco Luigde', *Publications of the Modern Language Association of* America 62 (1947), 887–909.

FURTHER READING

The medieval supernatural in Ireland and Wales: Williams, Mark, *Ireland's Immortals* (Princeton, NJ, 2016), chs. 1–6; Williams, Mark, *The Celtic Myths that Shape the Way We Think* (London, 2021). **Origins and development of ogam:**

Johnston, Elva, *Literacy and Identity in Early Medieval Ireland* (Cambridge, 2013); McManus, Damien, *A Guide to Ogam* (Maynooth, 1991). **Good online resources for ogam:** Ogam in 3D database (https://ogham.celt.dias.ie/); OG(H)AM Project (https://ogham.glasgow.ac.uk/).

AFTERLIVES

Translations of Iolo Morganwg: adapted from Williams ab Ithel, John (ed.), *Barddas: or, A collection of original documents, illustrative of the theology, wisdom, and usages of the Bardo-Druidic system of the isle of Britain (in English and Welsh),* vol. 1 (London, 1862), 360–61, 366–67.

FURTHER READING

Post-medieval interest in the Celts: Sims-Williams, Patrick, 'Celtomania and Celtoscepticism', *Cambrian Medieval Celtic Studies* 36 (1998), 1–36. Stewart, Ian, *The Celts: A Modern History* (Princeton, 2025). **John Dee and Welsh manuscripts:** Russell, Paul, '"Divers evidences antient of some Welsh princes": Dr John Dee and the Welsh context of the reception of Geoffrey of Monmouth in sixteenth-century England and Wales', in Hélène Tétrel and Géraldine Veysseyre (eds), *L'Historia regum Britannie et les «Bruts» en Europe, 2: Production, circulation et réception, XIIe-XVIe siècle* (Paris, 2018), 395–426. **Post-medieval history of druids and druidic ritual:** Hutton, Ronald, *Blood and Mistletoe: The History of the Druids in Britain* (London, 2009). **Romanticism and the Celtic Revival in Ireland and Scotland:** Williams, Mark, *Ireland's Immortals* (Princeton, NJ, 2016), chs. 7–12; see pp. 356–57 for the litany of the Order of the Celtic Mysteries. **Lady Wilde's claims about universal magic and druids:** Lady Wilde, *Ancient Cures, Charms, and Usages of Ireland: Contributions to Irish Lore* (London, 1890), 1, 9. **Witches, witchcraft, and pagan survival:** Hutton, Ronald, *The Triumph of the Moon: A History of Modern Pagan Witchcraft* (Oxford, 1999); Hutton, Ronald, *Queens of the Wild: Pagan Goddesses in Christian Europe: An Investigation* (New Haven, CT, 2023). **Neopaganism generally:** Magliocco, Sabina, 'Neopaganism', in Olav Hammer and Mikael Rothstein (eds), *The Cambridge Companion to New Religious Movements* (Cambridge, 2012), 150–66. **Stonehenge:** Hill, Rosemary, *Stonehenge* (London, 2008).

ACKNOWLEDGMENTS

Thanks to Mark Williams, Ben Hayes and India Jackson for suggesting that I write this book and to the editorial and production team at Thames & Hudson for their time, patience and creativity in bringing it to life. I am grateful to Brian Ehrmantraut, Thomas Nuckolls, Roan Runge, Eleanor Smith and James Drysdale Miller for their comments on earlier drafts and to my students at Cambridge for asking good questions in lectures. Thanks to David Stifter for sharing his forthcoming work on Irish charms.

SOURCES OF ILLUSTRATIONS

2 Prisma by Dukas Presseagentur GmbH/Alamy Stock Photo; **9** The Trustees of the British Museum; **13** Bibliothèque nationale de France, Paris. Photo BnF, Dist. GrandPalaisRmn/image BnF; **17** Musée de Cluny, Paris. akg-images/ Bildarchiv Steffens; **19** Musée de Cluny, Paris. GrandPalaisRmn (musée de Cluny - musée national du Moyen-Âge)/Gérard Blot, Jean-Gilles Berizzi; **20** National Museum of Denmark, Copenhagen. Photo Lennart Larsen/ National Museum DK Frederiksholms Channel 12 1220 Kbh. K Denmarm, C 6562-76; **22** Musée de Cluny, Paris. GrandPalaisRmn (musée de Cluny - musée national du Moyen-Âge)/Gérard Blot, Jean-Gilles Berizzi; **25** National Museums Scotland/Bridgeman Images; **27** Rijksmuseum, Amsterdam, BI-1917-383-21; **29** The Trustees of the British Museum; **32** Musée Archéologique de Dijon/ François Perrodin; **33** Musée Archéologique de Dijon/François Perrodin; **34** Musée Archéologique de Dijon/François Jay; **37** joserpizarro/Shutterstock; **38** The Art Institute Chicago, The Wallace L. DeWolf and Joseph Brooks Fair Collections, 1920.1930; **41** National Trust Images/Andreas von Einsiedel/ Bridgeman Images; **42** Drawn by R. E. M. Wheeler, collated by R.G.C., 1928. Reproduced from Lydney Report, by courtesy of the Society of Antiquaries; **43** Private Collection. Photo Look and Learn/Bridgeman Images; **44** David McQ /Alamy Stock Photo; **46** Jakub Rutkiewicz/Alamy Stock Photo; **49** Wellcome Collection, London; **50** Martin Bache/Alamy Stock Photo; **52** Image courtesy of the Centre for the Study of Ancient Documents (CSAD), University of Oxford, and the Roman Baths, Bath and North East Somerset Council; **55** Musee Bargoin, Clermont-Ferrand, France. Luisa Ricciarini / Bridgeman Images **56–57 (all)** Musée Bargoin, Clermont-Ferrand. Clermont Auvergne Métropole. Photo Jérôme Mondière; **59** Musée de Millau, Aveyron; **63** Hemis/Alamy Stock Photo; **67** Llyfrgell Genedlaethol Cymru – The National Library of Wales; **69** Rijksmuseum, Amsterdam, RP-P-1908-4557; **70 (both)** The Trustees of the British Museum; **73** Biblioteca Riccardiana, Florence. Luisa Ricciarini/Bridgeman Images; **76** Museo Archeologico Nazionale, Naples, Campania, Italy. Photo A. Dagli Orti/© NPL - DeA Picture Library/ Bridgeman Images; **79** Library of Congress, Washington D.C.; **80** The Trustees of the British Museum; **81** The Art Institute Chicago, Gift of Marilynn B. Alsdorf, 1991.375; **83** Private Collection; **84** Archivist/Adobe Stock; **85** The Art Institute Chicago, Mr. and Mrs. Potter Palmer Collection, 1926.75; **87** Private Collection. Stefano Bianchetti/Bridgeman Images; **88** Williamson Art Gallery & Museum, Birkenhead; **90** The Trustees of the British Museum; **92** S. R. Meyrick & C. H. Smith; **97** The Stapleton Collection/Bridgeman Images; **99** Office of Public Works, Dublin Castle; **100** National Museum of Ireland, Dublin. akg-images/Erich Lessing; **103** CPA Media Pte Ltd/Alamy Stock Photo; **104** Purchased 1946, National Galleries of Scotland, NG 2043; **105** National Museum of Ireland, Dublin; **106** Trinity College Dublin, MS 52;

107 (both) National Museum of Ireland, Dublin; **110** National Museum of Ireland, Dublin; **111** National Museum of Ireland, Dublin. akg-images/Manuel Cohen; **115** Trinity College Dublin, MS 58; **119** By permission of the Royal Irish Academy © RIA; **120** Wellcome Collection, London; **121** The Metropolitan Museum of Art, New York, The Jefferson R. Burdick Collection, Gift of Jefferson R. Burdick, 63.350.201.20.39; **123** Jesus College, Oxford, MS 111; **127** Pádraig Ó Macháin, University College Cork; **128 (all)** The Minneapolis Institute of Art, Gift of funds from Barbara S. Longfellow, 2015.51.1; **129 (left)** The New York Public Library Digital Collections, b14444147; **129 (right)** Wellcome Collection, London; **131** From the British Library archive/Bridgeman Images; **132** British Library, Cotton MS Vitellius C III; **135** Llyfrgell Genedlaethol Cymru – The National Library of Wales; **137 (all)** Zentralbibliothek, Zürich Ms. C 54; **142** Private Collection; **144** Photo By DEA/G. DAGLI ORTI/De Agostini via Getty Images; **145** From John Young Evans, Y llyfr cyntaf Pryderi fab Pwyll, 1922, Oxford University Press, London; **147** Dundee Art Galleries and Museums Collection (Dundee City Council), 178-1912; **148** Chronicle/Alamy Stock Photo; **151** Bequest of the artist 1946, National Galleries of Scotland, NG 2033; **152 (both)** From Ella Young and Maude Gonne, *The Coming of Lug: A Celtic Wonder-Tale*, 1909, Maunsel, Dublin; **155** Chronicle/Alamy Stock Photo; **156** T. W. Rolleston; **158** Newport Museum and Art Gallery/Bridgeman Images; **161** Natural History Museum, London; **165** Hulton Archive/Getty Images; **167** By permission of the Royal Irish Academy © RIA; **172 (above left)** National Library of Scotland, Oss.36; **172 (above right)** National Library of Scotland, Oss.37; **172 (below left)** National Library of Scotland, Oss.38; **172 (below right)** National Library of Scotland, Oss.39; **174** Harvard Art Museums/Fogg Museum, Gift of Belinda L. Randall from the collection of John Witt Randall, Photo President and Fellows of Harvard College, R5073; **176** Lyfrgell Genedlaethol Cymru – The National Library of Wales; **179** Llyfrgell Genedlaethol Cymru – The National Library of Wales; **180** Photo by George C. Beresford/Hulton Archive/Getty Images; **181** Keystone Press/Alamy Stock Photo; **182** National Gallery of Ireland, Dublin. GRANGER - Historical Picture Archive/Alamy Stock Photo; **184** From Ella Young and Maude Gonne, *The Coming of Lug: A Celtic Wonder-Tale*, 1909, Maunsel, Dublin; **185** From Ella Young and Maude Gonne, *The Coming of Lug: A Celtic Wonder-Tale*, 1909, Maunsel, Dublin; **187** Armagh County Museum Collection; **190** iLight photo/Adobe Stock; **193** Photo by Finnbarr Webster/Finnbarr Webster/Stringer/Getty Images

INDEX

Page numbers in *italics* refer to illustrations